# The God of HOPE

## A Daily Devotional for Hope

### SUSAN MAURER

WESTBOW
PRESS®
A DIVISION OF THOMAS NELSON
& ZONDERVAN

WestBow Press books may be ordered through booksellers or by contacting:

WestBow Press
A Division of Thomas Nelson & Zondervan
1663 Liberty Drive
Bloomington, IN 47403
www.westbowpress.com
844-714-3454

Scripture quotations taken from The Holy Bible, New International Version® NIV® Copyright ©
1973 1978 1984 2011 by Biblica, Inc. TM. Used by permission. All rights reserved worldwide.

Scripture quotations marked TPT are from The Passion Translation®. Copyright © 2017, 2018 by
Passion & Fire Ministries, Inc. Used by permission. All rights reserved. ThePassionTranslation.com.

Scripture quotations marked (NLT) are taken from the Holy Bible, New Living Translation,
copyright © 1996, 2004, 2007 by Tyndale House Foundation. Used by permission of
Tyndale House Publishers, Inc., Carol Stream, Illinois 60188. All rights reserved.

ISBN: 978-1-6642-2155-0 (sc)
ISBN: 978-1-6642-2156-7 (hc)
ISBN: 978-1-6642-2154-3 (e)

Library of Congress Control Number: 2021901730

Print information available on the last page.

WestBow Press rev. date: 02/01/2021

# Foreword

My name is Paula Hammontree. I worked in a gentleman's club for a number of years before I met Susan through the ministry team that goes into clubs like that to reach out to girls like me.

I knew my Bible, and I knew how to pray, but I had been in the dark so long I didn't want to pray. Susan began sending me prayers, daily. These prayers were so deep, so true to my life, and so profound I couldn't help but pray them aloud, pray them over my life, and finally, come into agreement with everything she prayed.

These daily prayers were real, raw, and unapologetic in that the only thing that mattered was our position with the Lord; having or being in the right position prayerfully with Christ Jesus brought everything into perspective: my relationships, my finances, restoration, love, forgiveness, and a cry for humility—everything a Christian should cry out for when I didn't know what to cry out for.

There were days, simply put, I did not feel like praying. Praying with Susan exposed those things inside me that kept me from going to the God of hope, the God of peace, and the God of joy.

I would wake up and look for her text/prayer, then pray over my life, agree with her, and add to her prayer because it provoked me. It wasn't enough to simply read the prayers. I found myself fully engaged with them.

I went as far as saving all the prayers, and then my phone was stolen. You can't imagen how disappointed I was to lose them. They were all precious to me because they were just as much a part of my life as they were hers. I often call her the prayer warrior; now I call her "Sis," but to me, she is both.

The Bible tells us, "Pray ye one for another that you may be healed."

And that's what I found: healing from the inside out!

## Dear Lord,

*Glory be to God and all the wonderful things He does in my life.*

*Lord, You are the great I Am. I praise You today and ask to see all Your goodness.*

*You shine Your light on me so I can see through the darkness and through all the confusion in front of me.*

*I will acknowledge Your blessings and glory with everything I do today.*

*Lord, be with me today to be a light to someone in darkness.*

*In Jesus's name, I pray.*

*Amen.*

# Dear Lord,

*You are our redeemer, our restorer, and creator of all things.*

*Your mercy and grace release us from the enemy, who tries to destroy us with his lies.*

*By You, we are completely forgiven, and in You we're declared perfectly righteous.*

*You are our reigning and returning king.*

*We are priceless and worthy because of the sacrifice You gave us of Your perfect life.*

*I sit in awe this morning of how blessed I am, not just for the prayers I pray but knowing that every single day You fight to bring us closer to You, Lord.*

*Let me know You better and love You unconditionally like You love us unconditionally.*

*In the name of Jesus, the Son of God. Amen.*

# Dear Lord,

Open my heart to hear Your message, and by faith, I'll accept Your direction and Word in my life.

I ask You, Lord, to show and deliver the Holy Spirit through me today. And by faith, I walk with You, to be Your hands and feet.

This day is Your gift to me. Let me not waste it but follow what You ask of me.

Give me the quiet moments today to reflect and listen.

In Jesus's name, I pray.

Amen.

# Dear Lord,

*Help us to never take Your sacrifice for granted. Forgive us for being too busy or distracted by other things and not fully recognizing what You freely have given and what You have done for us.*

*Thank You, for by Your wounds, we are healed. Our chains are gone if we choose them to be. Thank You for conquering the sin and letting Your power through the resurrection be everlasting.*

*We can say, "It is finished," and know that all forgiveness is ours if we just ask, that everything in our lives have been made new.*

*Lord, I give You all the glory!*

*In Jesus's name, I pray.*

*Amen.*

# Dear Lord,

*I know I belong to You. Please help me to understand who I am. Help me to hear the Holy Spirit and what He wants me to do today. My faith is strong. Still, in the quiet, I am surrounded by concern and doubt of what You want me to do.*

*Lord, I put all my concerns and doubts at Your feet. The enemy has no power over me. Your thoughts are higher than mine. Without You, I have nothing. But with You and through You, all things are possible. Show me the little things that You want me to do for Your glory, Lord, today and always.*

*In Jesus's name I pray.*

*Amen.*

> What, then, shall we say in response to these things? If God is for us, who can be against us? (Romans 8:31 NIV)

# Dear Lord,

*Thank You for all Your glory and compassion. Thy will be done. It can be so hard sometimes to let go, to not worry or wonder what's next. But Your grace and mercy wrap around me, and I know I am forgiven.*

*Your light is always there, even when it is so dark that I can't see the road before me. If I turn to You, Lord, and ask for Your guidance, my path becomes bright.*

*Lord, thank You for the new day to do Your work and be Your hands and feet.*

*In Jesus's name, I pray.*

*Amen.*

## Dear Lord,

*Give me patience and grace today. The enemy wants to tear down my trust and give me fear of the unknown. Lord, I know You are orchestrating my steps. I know You already know what I'm asking for. I know You always hear me. I know You always see me. Lord, please give me Your presence today and show me.*

*Let me hear You and see You at work and become a messenger of You. I know Your will is greater than my desires. I trust You, Lord, to help me get past those things that I cannot control and to look to You for comfort, not just things to satisfy my ego and flesh.*

*You are the great I Am!*

*In Your glorious name, Jesus, I pray.*

*Amen.*

## Dear Lord,

*I've learned that I may not be perfect or free from sin, but through You I am forgiven. Thank You, Lord, for so much You have given me.*

*Please give me Your strength and Your grace today to trust Your way and to trust the path You have in store for me, Lord.*

*Your love is overwhelming!*

*I know You have wonderful things in store for me. Give me the patience to wait on Your timetable, and not mine.*

*Please open the hearts of those around me to hear Your beautiful message. And show me where You are at work today so I may follow and help You.*

*In Jesus's name, I pray.*

*Amen.*

# Dear Lord,

My prayer to You is everything this morning, Lord.

You know what's in my heart. You already have my path. You've been so glorious and wonderful to me. I pray for grace today, to not let my ego and fears win. You are my Father, and You take care of all my needs. Glory be to God! I am silent and waiting.

Your will be done, Lord!

Let my heart and head have peace today with Your direction.

In Jesus's name, I pray.

Amen.

# Dear Lord,

*Thank You, Lord, for providing for me. The miracles that You give are answers to my prayers. To watch You move and comfort those who are priceless is why I worship You.*

*Lord, show me Your way today and help me walk on Your path.*

*I rebuke all negative and doubting thoughts that the enemy puts in my head. When I walk with You, no one can come against me. I trust in You with all my heart. Give me the quiet so I may hear Your messages for me and so that I will see where You are and I can join You.*

*In Jesus's name, I pray.*

*Amen.*

> For my Father's will is that everyone who looks to the Son and believes in him shall have eternal life and I will raise them up at that last day. (John 6:40 NIV)

# Dear Lord,

Lord, You are my hope. I invite the Holy Spirit to guide me today. I can get so caught up in the details when the enemy tries to alter my path. He wants me to stumble, and he likes it when I am confused and when I let him feed my ego. Lord, I rebuke everything that is put in my path that's not for my well-being, that's not directed by You or to You.

You already have my path outlined and built. Your ways are for me, not against me. It's Your will I want today to follow and obey.

Lord, show me how to be still and hear You, and show me how to open my eyes to Your work. I am grateful for Your love and devotion to me.

In Jesus's name, I pray.

Amen.

# Dear Lord,

*Lord, You are so amazing! Your love has shown me this morning the true love that I need to have for others. The hard and difficult part of my life is forgiven. All I need to do is love.*

*I know what You want me to do. I forgive those in my past, and I know that they were only doing the best that they could do. The people before them were not strong and loving.*

*Lord, be with me when I talk with them. Soften their hearts so they hear You through my words. You, Lord, are the highest power, and You are my Father.*

*Thank You, Jesus.*

*In Jesus's name I pray.*

*Amen.*

# Dear Lord,

*Be with me today. Fill me with Your Holy Spirit so I may have wisdom and patience toward others.*

*Please look over those in my life. I love them all.*

*Lord, I am Yours. Let me be Your hands and feet. Your will, not mine, will be done.*

*I give You all the glory in all the blessings You have given me and all the promises You will give me.*

*Help me walk in Your Word today and be a light to someone in darkness.*

*Show me Your plans, and I will obey You, Lord.*

*In Jesus's name, I pray.*

*Amen.*

## Dear Lord,

*Today is a beautiful day! Thank You for Your declaration of this day! Let me pray with others in Your name. Open our hearts to hear Your Word to us.*

*Lord, I hope that today I can reach one who is lost and needs the hope of You.*

*You give us so much strength, if we just let go and listen. You give us strength to step out of our comfort zones and reach the lost.*

*Let us be as faithful and loving to others as You are to us.*

*Lord, give us Your grace and wisdom today to forgive others of their sins to us and to forgive ourselves of our sins as You already have.*

*In Jesus's name, I pray.*

*Amen.*

He is my loving God and my fortress, my stronghold and my deliverer, my shield in who I take refuge, who subdues peoples under me. (Psalm 144:2 NIV)

# Dear Lord,

*Your promises to me are great. I see them as they come to me, and I'm so grateful. I know You want joy for me, and I ask You to give me the wisdom and the grace to not struggle with that but to accept all of it.*

*Lord, please put Your arms around all the people who need to see Your love. Open our hearts today, Lord, to hear Your message, to give us freedom from our fears, to rebuke the enemy and make him leave our daily lives. The enemy is not wanted here! I make room for Your love. Let us all become Your fruit and be fruitful today in Your name, Jesus!*

*In Jesus's name, I pray.*

*Amen.*

> He upholds the cause of the oppressed and gives food to the hungry. The Lord sets prisoners free, the Lord gives sight to the blind, the Lord lifts up those who are bowed down, the Lord loves the righteous. (Psalms 146:7 NIV)

## Dear Lord,

*You are the great I Am! Your grace wins every time. Lord, let me release my fears and worries to You today. I let go.*

*I will put on the belt of truth and the breastplate of righteousness and raise Your shield of faith. I will spread Your Gospel of peace to someone today.*

*Lord, I ask for Your hedge of protection for my family today. Let them see and fear no evil.*

*Your love and guidance in our lives directs us to what is good and just.*

*Thank you, Lord, for all Your blessings!*

*In Jesus's name, I pray.*

*Amen.*

## Dear Lord,

May nothing separate me from You today. Teach me to choose only Your way, so that every step I take will lead me closer to You.

Help me walk in Your Word today and not my own feelings. Help me to keep my heart pure and undivided. Protect me from my own thoughts, words, and actions that are careless.

Keep me from being distracted by my wants, my desires, and my thoughts of how I think it should be.

Help me to embrace all things that come my way as an opportunity instead of an inconvenience. And help me to rest in Your truth.

You already see the ways I will fall short and mess up. But right now, I will tuck Your whispers and Word of absolute truth and love for me into my heart.

I know Your love for me is not something that is earned. It's not based on my performance. You love me just the way I am. That's amazing to me. What's also amazing is that my Savior, who is also the Savior of the world, wants to spend time with me every morning.

Lord, help me to remember what a gift it is to spend time with You.

In Jesus's name, I pray.

Amen.

## Dear Lord,

*Thank you, Lord, for all the blessings You have given me and all that You have promised.*

*Help me to fix my eyes on You, Lord, so that in all my decisions and all my actions, it is You who is directing them. With this, I let go of all my concerns and burdens.*

*Lord, I am only Your servant. Teach me to be more of a servant for those in need—not just those I see every day but those I may see for the first time.*

*Help me to be a blessing in that person's eyes, to take Your message outside my comfort zone.*

*I receive so much love and goodness from You. Let me show others that same love and goodness.*

*It's for Your glory that I want to become a better representative of all that You are, Lord.*

*In Jesus's name, I pray.*

*Amen.*

# Dear Lord,

*Bless all those who haven't seen Your glory. Lord, Your Holy Spirit is welcome. Please wrap me in Your Holy Spirit today and give me the peace I need. My promise to You is to listen to the still, small voice that You speak to me, to honor without questioning Your wisdom and mercy for me today, to speak the words You have for me so that others are encouraged, so that when I speak, they hear You, Lord.*

*Let me show others my acknowledgment of You. You are the way, the light, and my truth! Lord, You amaze me with everything You do and will do in my life.*

*In Jesus's name, I pray.*

*Amen.*

I have learned the secret of being content in any and every situation, whether well fed or hungry, whether living in plenty or in want. I can do all this through Him, who gives me strength. (Philippians 4:12 NIV)

# Dear Lord,

*Forgive me of my sins today and forgive those who will sin against me.*

*Lord, You are the light on my path. Be with me today. I am stronger with You near me. I can do all things through You. Be the words that come out of my mouth, so I can speak Your goodness to others. The enemy tries to move between us, but I declare that he has no room.*

*Your grace, Lord, is what I need today to listen to others and not judge, to be a light to them. It is Your will, Lord, not mine. I let go of all control. Your ways are higher and better than mine. With all my heart, I trust in You.*

*In Jesus's name, I pray.*

*Amen.*

Put your hope in God for I will yet praise Him, my savior and my God. (Psalms 42:5 NIV)

## Dear Lord,

*Thank You for showing me Your glory this week. Please give me wisdom today so I can see Your answers to problems that You put in front of me. It's Your plan and Your will, Lord.*

*Your presence will be felt in all that I do.*

*You put words in my mouth when I spoke. Please bless those who don't see Your goodness and light.*

*Lord, bless the lost one.*

*Please open the door so they can see Your love and forgiveness. They hurt inside and need Your arms around them. Show them once more that they are forgiven. Bring them peace and strength to fight the enemy that threatens to torture them. Lord, You are good to everything that we come across today. Teach us that it's all for Your glory and our good.*

*In Jesus's name, I pray.*

*Amen.*

> Now faith is confidence in what we hope for and assurance about what we do not see. (Hebrews 11:1 NIV)

# Dear Lord,

*Thank You for Your gift of mercy and forgiveness. Lead me on Your path today with wisdom and patience. I know there are things I can't see that You have planned. Your ways are much higher than I can ever think. Please bless those who are in need of Your love and spirit. Guide us to do Your deeds unselfishly and in Your name, that we can see others around us who may need that word of encouragement. Give us that word today so that we can show others You are at work.*

*In Jesus's precious name, I pray.*

*Amen.*

> "Peace I leave with you; my peace I give you. I do not give to you as the world gives. Do not let your hearts be troubled and do not be afraid." (John 14:27 NIV)

## Dear Lord,

*Forgive those who are blind to Your true ways and are not able to see Your light.*

*Lord, please show me the light of Your way, Your truth, so that I can give it to someone who needs Your good Word.*

*Lord, let me be patient and deliberate before speaking out. Show me how to be still and listen, to be humble in Your presence, to be a rock to someone in need. Lord, I know You hear my prayers, and in Your time, Your will be done. Lord, please heal those who are hurting so that they can see Your glory and goodness. Show them the light of Your path too.*

*Lord, thank You for all Your wonderful blessings in my life.*

*Without You, I am nothing and I have nothing. It's for Your glory forever in all that I do!*

*In Jesus's name, I pray.*

*Amen.*

> I pray that the eyes of your heart may be enlightened in order that you may know the hope to which he has called you, the riches of His glorious inheritance in His holy people, and His incomparably great power for us who believe. (Ephesians 1:18 NIV)

# Dear Lord,

*Please make us more like You, Lord. Please open our hearts to Your message. Help us truly love one another, not just to say it but to truly have the self-forgetful love. Let us see and feel that You want us to be forgiving and patient with one another. It's so easy to hide in Your Word as a barrier to our journey toward You. Lord, humble us and give us the strength to step out of that barrier and face our challenges, our giants, with confidence that You are with us. Just reading Your words, Lord, isn't what You want us to do. You don't want us to become false prophets. I know You ask us to live Your Word in our actions, to love all our brothers and sisters, no matter the circumstance.*

*Lord, let them see You in me and rebuke all fear that the enemy tries to put in our ears. The enemy cannot touch our hearts. Please, Lord, give us the strength to humble ourselves and not boast of our deeds through You.*

*Lord, please give hope and faith to those who are lost. They read Your Word but have distance in their lives. Bring them closer, Lord.*

*In Jesus's name, I pray.*

*Amen.*

## Dear Lord,

*Please be with me today. Let the Holy Spirit guide me in what Your will is. Let my heart be pure and honest and hear only You.*

*I know that it's so easy to be overcome and trust that my wants are Your wants, when in fact they aren't. Or I keep trying to push a feeling or a way, but at the end of it is a wall, a dead end.*

*If I can just be still and let go, You will guide my path. If I can be patient when you're quiet, find glory in Your tests, and obey Your Word. Lord, Your ways are higher and better than my ways.*

*Lord, thank You for all Your blessings in my life, those in the past and those You have promised me that are yet to come. Let me continue to have a love relationship with You, no matter what is in my life, to be Your messenger in the world.*

*In Jesus's name, I pray.*

*Amen.*

> Look to the Lord and his strength; seek his face always. Remember the wonders he has done. (Psalm 105:4–5 NIV)

## Dear Lord,

*Please give me patience today. It's so easy to get frustrated with the world and things around me. Lord, I know You see things I can't see, and You know things I don't know. When things feel like they are spinning out of control, I can get caught up in all of it. Please guide me to be still in the storm, to see Your work going on around me. Let me be like Elisha. Let me see the angel army on the hill.*

*I know You are with me every step of the way, that all I have to do is stop and be still.*

*Lord, You are the great I Am, the one who overcomes, the sovereign Lord to us all.*

*Thank You, Lord, for Your grace and mercy today.*

*In Jesus's name, I pray.*

*Amen.*

# Dear Lord,

*Glory be to God! Your mercy and grace are all we need. We get off track and forget that from time to time when we go out into the world. It would be the perfect world if all we did was pray on Your Word all day long. But that is not what You want, is it? We have to put on our armor and step out, to show our hope to others who don't have Your hope, to have faith that what You say will be done is done, to give love to others the same way You show us love every day.*

*To be strong in Your Word and rebuke the enemy.*

*To listen to the Holy Spirit as He guides us throughout the day.*

*Glory be to God and all Your goodness!*

*In Jesus's name, I pray.*

*Amen.*

## Dear Lord,

*I know that we can come to You in our suffering and give it all to You, because You too share in our sufferings. Everything that we go through, You already know.*

*They are Your battles to fight.*

*Teach us to give glory to You, to bless You always and be with You. Without You, we are not blessed.*

*Lord, Your words to us are always what we need to hear. Thank You for our grace and mercy in our lives.*

*You fill us up every day to go out and find where You are at work. To find the one who may be lost.*

*Lord, thank You for blessing our families. Just being in one another's presence gives us strength in Your name. Open our eyes and hearts, Lord, to Your love.*

*In Jesus's name, I pray.*

*Amen.*

# Dear Lord,

Lord, it is so easy to ask for forgiveness, and then we expect almost clear thinking the rest of the day. But that never happens. We are constantly faced with personal challenges. Lord, please give me Your grace and Your wisdom today to forgive myself and remember who You say we are and not who the enemy says we are.

Lord, we want to live in the Spirit and hear Your still, small voice, Your whispers, not live for what pleases us on the outside.

We want to do Your work, to walk with You, to be Your hands and feet, to have peace and Your love. Lord, please bless us with Your peace and love today.

Lord, let us rebuke what the enemy wants us to think and feel and only focus on You and Your goodness and love.

In Jesus's name, I pray.

Amen.

## Dear Lord,

*Today we ask for Your mercy on those who are lost and needing Your forgiveness. Let them forgive themselves. Lord, they are so broken, and they need to feel Your love. Please break down the walls they have built to hide in the darkness. Light up their worlds so nothing can hide, so no enemy can continue to plot against them, Lord. In Your name, we declare victory over their lives.*

*Lord, show us to pray in hope, to not grieve but to celebrate Your powerful love.*

*You said to us, "God is love." Show us how to love these ones who have gone astray and not judge them by their actions, to love the person and hate the actions, to help them forgive themselves and not let feelings stand in the way of receiving all Your blessings.*

*Lord, these are Your children. All of them were made in Your image. All of them have love in their hearts. Help give them strength to rebuke the enemy and break their chains, to walk in Your light with absolutely no shame.*

*It's in Jesus's name, we pray for the one.*

*Amen.*

# Dear Lord,

*I come before You this morning knowing that all control is in Your hands. It is Your will that is done. I know, Lord, that You care for all Your people, not just the ones who appear to be perfect in every way.*

*Lord, right now, there is one who is struggling with a difficult trial. I can see their strength faltering, Lord, and I know that You have all the strength they need.*

*I pray that You will reach down and touch the one right now wherever they are at this moment. Please let Your presence fill the room where they are at and let them feel an extra portion of Your strength to help them get through the day.*

*They need You now, Lord. Thank You, Lord, for blessing them and loving them during their difficult time.*

*In Jesus's name, I pray.*

*Amen.*

Do you not know? Have you not heard? The Lord is the everlasting God. The creator of the ends of the earth. He will not grow tired or weary and His understanding no one can fathom. He gives strength to the weary and increases the power of the weak. (Isaiah 40:28–29 NIV)

# Dear Lord,

*I choose joy—joy unending that comes from lingering longer in Your presence, staying in peace with the Holy Spirit, and remembering Your Word throughout the day. Please draw my heart closer to Yours, Lord, that You are always the first person I run to when my cup is empty. All of what You give me is Yours, and all of what I see is Yours. You are the one I run to first with good news and celebration. It's all for Your glory, Lord.*

*In Jesus's name, I pray.*

*Amen.*

## Dear Lord,

*Lord, give me patience today when things before me don't seem to be answered, for solutions that aren't there, to know that every decision and solution passes through Your hands, to know that You are still on the throne. Give me the grace and the wisdom to constantly seek Your counsel when I don't know why something happens.*

*Lord, let me by Your conduit to someone in need, that they may hear You through my words today, that the Holy Spirit flows through me to give someone comfort and hope.*

*The glory of Your love is always enough when I'm impatient and confused. Once I turn to You, Lord, I know You will accept my burdens and stress. Lord, we give thanks for the test that You give us to be closer to You.*

*Lord, we will wait patiently and stand firm in the truth of Your Word.*

*In Jesus's name, I pray.*

*Amen.*

> Come, let us sing for joy to the Lord … let us come before him with thanksgiving. (Psalm 95:1–2 MEV)

# Dear Lord,

*You are the great healer, our God of hope and mercy. Please look down on those hurt and touch them with Your right hand. Touch their wounds that they may be healed. Your angels surround them now and protect them. Lord, we need You. We lift up to You our praise of Glory to God in the highest, our thankfulness for all You do, for all You teach us. We are Your love, Lord, made in Your likeness.*

*Lord, this morning, we let You lavish us with Your good and powerful love. We sit in Your presence, sending all that love to the ones who are hurting, that they will be healed in Your name. Lord, stay by their side and comfort them in Your arms.*

*Lord, bless them with the healing that only You can give.*

*In Jesus's name, I pray.*

*Amen.*

## Dear Lord,

*Thank You for this day. Thank You for this time to spend with You this morning. You are so patient. My love for You is so strong, but I constantly doubt myself. I know that through You, all things are possible. You are my rock, my cornerstone, my adamancy. You alone will fight my battles and direct my steps in light. You know where You want me to go. I trust in You!*

*Lord, please quiet my mind, all the noise and guilt that is in there today. Please release me. It's only the insignificant enemy that tries to gain a hold of me and pick at my weaknesses. I'm feeling a little lost today. Give me Your strength to open the door when You knock. I claim the Holy Spirit to surround me with Your love and protection.*

*In Jesus's name, I decree that angel armies are loosed. I decree that God's ways are fixed and unmovable! I decree God's Word of truth will be my testimony!*

*In Jesus's name, I pray.*

*Amen.*

# Dear Lord,

*Deliver me from the evil one who tries to tear at my thoughts and my strength in You, who tries to give me doubts in all that I do during the day. Lord, I rebuke all that the dark tries to say and walk in Your light.*

*Your truth is all I need. Lord, I ask for healing for those in pain today, both mentally and physically. They can trust You, Lord, to point them on Your path. We can all turn to You and fix our eyes on Your face. Your Holy Spirit will guide us and test us. We won't lose faith or hope in what the Holy Spirit asks us to do.*

*Lord, give us patience to wait for Your direction, to stay faithful and hopeful in the quiet times. Lord, teach us to be mindful of our tongues and become wiser in Your Word.*

*In Jesus's name, I pray.*

*Amen.*

> May the God who gives endurance and encouragement give you the same attitude of mind toward each other that Christ Jesus had. (Romans 15:5 NIV)

# Dear Lord,

*I pray for all who need You today. Show them the way. Lord, You are the truth, the way, and the life. All who come to You with open hearts will receive Your love. You are always there waiting for us, aren't You? Waiting for us to turn to You and accept You into our lives. Reading Your scripture and trying to fit it into our lives is not Your plan for us, but rather to let You guide us to Your Holy Spirit's message. Each of us have our own message from You. Your message is far more important than our thoughts, and to obey Your Word is so important; to let go of what we think, to stop trying to manipulate how we want our lives to go, to surrender to what You want us to do.*

*Lord, we know it is confusing and sometimes uncomfortable for us to be still and know, to step out of our comfort zone. You ask us to deny ourselves, take up our crosses, and follow You. And each day, we try, but that is all You ask of us. Every morning, we should be still and listen to Your Word, Your truth, to give all our worries and wasteful concerns and thoughts to You. We pray for guidance to reach out and help someone today, to stretch out of our comfort zone.*

*In Jesus's name, we pray.*

*Amen.*

# Dear Lord,

*Thank You for Your blessings, those that I've seen and those yet to come.*

*Lord, I lift up the hurting to You, those witnesses and servants of Your love, that they may find rest and hope in Your arms. You are our sovereign, Lord, and everything is possible through You. We have hope in You. We are not forsaken. Give us the strength and confidence to trust the hope and to know You are still and always will be on the throne.*

*Remind us every day to put on our full armor of God, our breastplate of righteousness, our belt of truth, our helmet of salvation, our feet with the Gospel. Help us pick up the shield of faith and the sword of Your Word.*

*Lord, help us to hold on to the Holy Spirit who guides us.*

*We give You all the glory.*

*In Jesus's name, I pray.*

*Amen.*

How precious, O God, is your constant love,! We find protection under the shadow of your wings. (Psalm 36:7 GNT)

# Dear Lord,

*You are the glory of my blessings each day. Lord, please send mercy and grace to those who are in need today, those who are hurting and confused. Give them Your comfort and show them how merciful You are. Let me be still today and listen for Your words. Lord, please bless me with Your wisdom and the grace I need to say the right things at the right time, with conviction and not opinion, never scolding or self-righteous but humble and soft. Let my journey today be valuable to someone in need.*

*Lord, You are the great Yahweh, our healer and sovereign Lord. Be with Your faithful servants in their time of need for healing and show those who are not yet Your believers how good You are!*

*In Jesus's name, I pray.*

*Amen.*

# Dear Lord,

*What a beautiful day to take Your message to someone in need. We will wait for You to show us where You want us to be. We know that You will reveal to us where You are at work. We don't need to quote Your words but to speak through the Holy Spirit, and sometimes that means being silent and listening.*

*Lord, thank You for the blessings You have given us. Please go with me today and find the one who needs Your message, that Your words through me will lift them up. Lord, I ask for Your protection and Your light as we go before evil, that the enemy will see You and fear You, that we will bring light to the broken and hurting, to let them know they are priceless, they are loved, and they are forgiven.*

*In Jesus's name, I pray.*

*Amen.*

# Dear Lord,

We are so blessed today, Lord! Forgive me of my sins today and please forgive those who will sin against me.

Lord, thank You for all Your goodness, for allowing me and choosing me to shed light where there is darkness. Lord, please show me Your mercy and grace when dealing with my own thoughts and judgments. Help me understand quickly that it is never I who should speak or think judgment on another person, even when it is gossip or opinions I hear, even if I know what I hear is against Your name. Teach me to take the plank out of my eye first before pointing out the spec in someone else's eye.

Lord, please transform me to be humbled in my walk and to begin with my own issues and chose to live the truth in Your holy name.

Lord, take me by the hand and lead me into a radical life change. I want every part of my life to be a message that points others to You. I want to know You for who You are rather than what You are against. I will no longer make excuses. Convict me of the areas that contradict Your work in my life.

In Jesus's name, I pray.

Amen.

# Dear Lord,

*Thank You for giving me this day. Let me be thankful even when there are challenges.*

*Lord, I know You hear me. You show me Your favor. You have protected me through my whole life. I know You walk with me every day to help make my paths straight.*

*Lord, I pray that Your angel armies protect all those who are innocent and need help, that they can turn to You soon to be a light in their darkness, to be a witness to Your love and mercy.*

*Lord, I need Your grace to know the right words of wisdom today, to not be slanderous or negative toward anyone or anything, to not be boastful but to be humbled in Your name.*

*Lord, give me strength to accomplish all that You want me to do for You.*

*You energize my mind and my soul every day and make me want to search for You and spend all day in Your presence. I need to put on my armor and become one of Your warriors in the world.*

*Lord, it is Your will that is done. Your ways are better and higher than mine.*

*In Jesus's name, I pray.*

*Amen.*

# Dear Lord,

*I pray that You will give me Your grace to deal with anything that comes my way today.*

*Lord, I know Your Holy Spirit was with me last night while I slept. You give me such peace. I ask for guidance in my prayers to know where You want me. Your will be done. Lord, please give me the wisdom to discern those moments when things do not go as I asked or prayed. Lord, I do ask for healing on the ones that I name in prayer, that Your arms will hold them while they heal. I declare You will open good treasure over us all and rain it down upon us. The blood of Jesus washes over us all. We celebrate You and all Your glory. You are our Father and maker of all things. We will never forsake that.*

*In Jesus's name, I pray.*

*Amen.*

## Dear Lord,

Lord I praise You this morning for all Your goodness and blessings. Lord, let me be humbled and not proud today. Let me pause and ponder You.

Open my eyes to Your work and messages around me. Let me hear Your still voice. Give me Your wisdom, Lord, to not be boastful in myself but to be boastful in You.

Lord, I take up my cross today and follow You. You are my guide, even when I think I am alone. I will remind myself that You are near me always.

Lord, please give me Your thoughts and the Holy Spirit that comforts me and gives me strength. I am nothing without You.

I am fruitless if I do not have love for others, if I do not have love in my heart.

Lord, thank You for Your compassion as I continue to grow closer to You, even when I mess up, as I learn what You want me to do and where You want me to go. Even in the quiet season, I know I am Your child.

In Jesus's name, I pray.

Amen.

## Dear Lord,

*You are worthy, Lord. To You all the glory for what happens today and for healing the sick and hurt.*

*Lord, I can never forget Your power and the grace in all that You do. I am blessed in Your name. Lord, give me the patience to understand the salvation I have received in Your name, to learn each day what it means and to listen as I learn and hear Your Word.*

*Lord, give me Your mercy when I get inpatient while I wait in silence, to know that Your love always surrounds me. I walk in faith, Lord, with no fear because You are beside me. You are near me if I stumble and quick to catch me with Your love.*

*Lord, I praise You with all my soul. I ask for Your continued healing miracles for those who are suffering. In Jesus's name, I pray.*

*Amen.*

> Love the Lord your God with all your heart and with all your soul and with all you strength. (Deuteronomy 6:5 NIV)

## Dear Lord,

*I praise You! Let me rest in You and trust in Your grace through faith. I rest in the fact that You are my comforter and counselor. Today I will be on Your path, not my own. I know that all my faith and hope won't cause any storms to disappear, but Your strength fills the gap in my weakness. Lord, be greater than my heart. I put my hope in You, my source of all things. Be still my soul and let me realize that You are my strength in every occasion, my source of all power. Reveal in me the ways that will help me grow more ferocious in my faith. Give me Your supernatural favor and joy. Help my heart and soul to not only embrace and cling to the truth, that You find me worthy of Your favor and joy, but to deeply receive it in Your name and for Your glory. Continue to move me, to push me forward with the passion that only the Holy Spirit can give. Let me complete my passion with praises of Your goodness and creation.*

*In Jesus's name, I pray.*

*Amen.*

## Dear Lord,

*I praise Your goodness and mercy. Please give me peace in my mind and calm my anxious heart. Be still my soul when I can't find my balance. When I worry about things out of my control, shift my thoughts out of the negative, crazy spiraling thoughts and teach me to practice taking them captive and practicing the never-ending faith in You. May the focus be solely on You.*

*Give me the strength and clarity of mind to walk only on the path You have laid out for me.*

*I trust Your love, God, and I know You heal all stress. The sun will rise each day to block out the darkness. Let my eyes see the light in every moment, the light that is You.*

*In Jesus's name, I pray.*

*Amen.*

## Dear Lord,

*I choose today to take every thought captive because I know that You are more powerful than my thoughts, my circumstances, and any fears that threaten me.*

*I know that I can stand firm and trust Your process because the benefits of doing so will far outweigh what I can see. The enemy cannot distract me because I am eternally secure in You. I declare the Gospel fearlessly! Thank You, Jesus!*

*In Jesus's name, I pray.*

*Amen.*

## Dear Lord,

*Thank You, Lord, for all Your blessings in my life, from the safety You give me to the peace I feel with You.*

*I know Your strength is like the oceans, deep and powerful and never-ending, but at the same time, You are peaceful and constant like the sound of the waves when they lap the shores.*

*Lord, I crucify my flesh and surrender to Your will. I trust in You and hold my peace close. My foundation is in You, the peace that transcends every situation. It is peace that only the Holy Spirit can deliver, peace that is active and gives me a confident trust, no matter what's going on around me.*

*I stand firm in Your light. You guide me, mature me, and strengthen me in my weakness. Forgive the sins I've committed and forgive those who sin against me. Expose the area in my heart that lacks peace so that I can grow in Your wisdom.*

*Lord, lead my thoughts, my actions, and my heart today. Your guided restraint and self-control will lead my pathway and my steps.*

*In Jesus's name, I pray.*

*Amen.*

## Dear Lord,

*Glory to God! Let us praise You for Your goodness!*

*Lord, forgive me of my sins. I know I've been frustrated during this time. I should not judge why others behave the way they do or gather things. This too shall pass. Help me remember to bless them because I don't know what they are facing.*

*Lord, remind me that You are always in charge. You have never been out of control. Your actions always bring eternal blessings to me. Remind me of Your truths.*

*You are sovereign. You are our provider. You made me and have me in the palm of Your hand. You have a purpose for me, and You have a place for me to fulfill that purpose. Let me listen to You and fix my eyes only on You so I can have and carry the inner peace that comes only from You.*

*In Jesus's name, I pray.*

*Amen.*

God is our refuge and strength, an ever present help in trouble. (Psalms 46:1 NIV)

## Dear Lord,

*I praise You for all the wonderful things You have done for me, the redemptive work You have given me. Lord, give me strength today to not breathe life into the chaos that tries to surround me. Let me forgive others as You forgave me. Let me understand what it is to feel the power of the resurrection through the Holy Spirit that is in me, to know You are in control. As it is written, transform me by the renewing of my mind constantly. Let me continue to hold captive the thoughts that threaten not to lead me to peace today. I choose to refocus my mind, to trust You in every circumstance and situation I face. You alone assure me inner peace. I will focus only on what's lovely, noble, praiseworthy, and pleasant. I choose to live in hope. Through faith in what is unseen, I have hope, and hope is the anchor to my soul—firm and secure.*

*In Jesus's name, I pray.*

*Amen.*

## Dear Lord,

I praise You and thank You for all Your blessings. Lord, forgive me when I judge others' actions or nonactions. I know that every time I do this, I'm playing into the chaos that threatens my peace, the peace that comes only from You. Let me march toward my Jerusalem with the promise of God in my heart.

Lord, please guide me to help others, to be sacrificial and not selfish, to put others first. Let me spend my time praising You for Your goodness and not worrying about things here on earth.

Lord, Your will be done, not mine. Give us wisdom and discernment today.

In Jesus's name, I pray.

Amen.

## Dear Lord,

*I love and praise You with deep prayer, so that when any problems come my way, I can stand in Your grace and be unshaken and empowered, keeping my eyes on You. You have promised to work all things for my good. I give You all my problems today, which You, the God who created the universe, can handle.*

*Forgive me for focusing on things, good and bad, and not You, for not keeping my eyes on You always. My problems and concerns are so small compared to You.*

*Lord, I know You are using this time to help the one to see Your power and strength in the midst of the darkness. Lord, I praise You for all the positive things that have come out of this brief moment in time:*

- *Parents are spending more time with their children.*
- *We are reassessing what is most important in our lives.*
- *Kindness is winning over selfishness.*
- *People are turning to You for their answers.*
- *We are appreciating the little things that we took for granted: a hug, a handshake, whispers, sharing a meal or a cup of coffee with a friend.*

*May our Lord always remind us of how good He is!*

*In Jesus's name, I pray.*

*Amen.*

# Dear Lord,

*Forgive us our sins. Remind us to bless others and not curse or judge them, not to let the fear and anxiety they are dealing with overshadow love.*

*Lord, let Your love clothe us, cover us, and heal us. By Your will, fill us with peace, thanksgiving, and gratitude.*

*Remind us that we are the light that can overcome evil with good, that we will place others above ourselves. We will not lose hope in the Gospel. Guard our hearts for only Your wisdom, rebuking any small bit of evil that tries to take hold.*

*Lord, let us worship You so our mouths, our minds, our imaginations, and our whole beings are only focused on You. Let us be love, the love that is defined only by You as sacrificial, unmerited deeds to help a person in need, the type of love that supersedes all gifts and outlasts them all.*

*In Jesus's name, I pray.*

*Amen.*

> For I know the plans I have for you, declares the Lord, "plans to prosper you and not harm you, plans to give you hope and a future." (Jeremiah 29:11 NIV)

# Dear Lord,

*We praise You! We have renewed hope through Jesus Christ every day. We rejoice in You with gratitude and thanksgiving. Your greatness and awesomeness are more than we will ever imagine.*

*Lord, You are trustworthy and true. You teach us every day that we can always depend on You and lean on You. You promise us wisdom and peace if we come to You with an open heart. Let us open the eyes of our hearts to see what You want for us today, to look beyond ourselves.*

*Lord, grant us Your grace, which exceeds what we deserve, the grace that Jesus bought for us with His life and sacrifice.*

*Lord, it's Your mercy for us that You show us daily, with forgiveness always. We ask Your Holy Spirit to fill us so we can work Your purposes through our daily deeds. During this storm, let us be still and hear only You.*

*In Jesus's name, I pray.*

*Amen.*

## Dear Lord,

*Thank You, Jesus, for all Your mercies and grace. Thank You for this gift of time we all have. Thank You that the sun will rise today, for all the blessings You will give us, for the joy, peace, and hope that I can claim and own.*

*Lord, forgive me of doubt. Forgive me of my pride. Let me rest in You. I will deny myself today, take up my cross, and follow You. Give me the strength to rebuke all the little lies, the chaos that threatens to surround me, and focus on You.*

*Lord, I am grateful for Your grace finding me and filling me with the Holy Spirit each day.*

*Lord, forgive those who open themselves to the negative and refuse to see the opportunity that You have given us. Heal any gaps with the patience to accept the things we cannot change. Help us turn to You in this and every moment.*

*In Jesus's name, I pray.*

*Amen.*

Be kind and compassionate to one another, forgiving each other, just as in Christ God forgave you. (Ephesians 4:32 NIV)

# Dear Lord,

Thank You for Your grace, for the unity we can have with one another as believers in You and in Your Holy Spirit. Thank You for providing a way for each of us to be united and one in You. Help us to live each day in the unity of and encouragement for one another so we can glorify You.

Lord, this morning, You showed me that Your love cannot be measured. You stretched Your arms over the ocean and said it is wider than any ocean, deeper than any ocean, and more powerful than any ocean's strength. You told me that our love for one another should mirror Your love for us.

Lord, forgive us when we forget this. When pride sneaks in and takes over, let us pause and remember to glorify You in everything we do and to know You are in control.

In Jesus's name, I pray.

Amen.

## Dear Lord,

*Thank You for this day to remember and honor You. Lord, as this day goes on, remind me to pause and pray on all that You did for me. Don't let the chaos and the busyness of the day drown out the glory and magnitude of the price You paid for me. Let me honor You not just for today but for every day You give me. Thank You that by Your wounds, I am healed, that by Your sacrifice, I am free. Thank You, Jesus, that Your power is everlasting. Thank You, Lord, that with hope and faith, I can believe "It is finished."*

*In Jesus's name, I pray for peace for all.*

*Amen.*

## Dear Lord,

*Thank You for Your love, for Your sacrifice. Fill me this morning to overflowing with Your Holy Spirit. Remind me that only You are in control. Let me be broken and poured out, to relinquish control completely. Let me not always be comfortable with those who also see You but be bold in the name of Jesus and share the good news of Your resurrection. Let Your love overcome any fears or obstacles. To God be all the glory.*

*Lord, Your mercies and grace overwhelm me daily. Lord, I declare that Your angel armies are released to protect and surround the one. Give them Your strength to defeat any challenges that come their way. Let me be Your hands and feet today, Lord.*

*In Jesus's name, I pray.*

*Amen.*

The only thing that counts is faith expressing itself through love. (Galatians 5:6 NIV)

## Dear Lord,

*You are awesome! We praise You. We give thanks for all the new things we are able to see and hear. You open doors. You right every wrong. You always go before us. You are behind and beside us. Lord, renew my hope today. Reveal what is in my heart by opening the eyes of my heart. Cleanse me, Lord.*

*Not by my will but Your will be done!*

*In Jesus's name, I pray.*

*Amen.*

*Dear Lord,*

*Thank You for being the God of restoration, for making all things new each day. Thank You for being the author of our faith and working all things for our good. There is nothing You don't control, nothing You don't see. Lord, keep my eyes fixed only on You, the perfecter of hope. Be still my soul and forgive me for trying to control things. Let me place my hope in You, wiping away any worries or fear. Restore my joy and faith in Your greatness, not in my circumstances. Help me to live as a light and witness to Your truth. Help me to live and love in a way that honors You each day. Free me from any enslavement to my circumstances and instead rest my hope and heart in only You.*

*In Jesus's powerful name, I pray!*

*Amen.*

If I do a really scary thing, like surrender my life
completely to Jesus, what will I get?
His peace that's impenetrable.
His joy that's indescribable.
His freedom that's unexplainable.
His love that's outrageous.
His mercy that's generous.
His grace that's undeserving.
His presence that's soothing.
His wisdom that's reassuring.
More of Him, less of me!

## Dear Lord,

*Thank You for all things that You have given me, from my ability to see and hear all that You created to the will of my decisions each day. Thank You for who You have put in my path, my Christian family that loves and supports one another. You give me the desire to give back to You. You provide for me and give me the desire to know and believe You will always provide for me if I put my faith exclusively in You. Forgive me of my sins and forgive those who sin against me.*

*Lord, teach me to always conform to Your truth and to communicate Your truth to others who want to know You. Let me know the by-products, faith and love, from the hope I have in You. Teach me to be still and know.*

*Help me to have the faith that my soul looks upward, the love that my soul looks outward, and the hope that my soul looks forward. Let me be more like Jesus with hands that care, feet that are on solid ground, and a heart overflowing.*

*In Jesus's name, I pray.*

*Amen.*

*Dear Lord,*

*Thank You for Your Word, for Your Holy Spirit, and for other believers who surround me. Lord, constantly search my heart to reveal to me those walls that build inside my heart and keep me from being closer to You. Lord, guide me to walk closer to You today. Show me what I need to do to demonstrate my trust in You. Help me find Your peace, to be able to show and feel Your overwhelming peace in every circumstance. Give me Your wisdom that I need to overcome every situation. Let me bless and love others, to believe in them and always hope for the best for them, to consider things from their point of view. Help me to apologize when I need to right a wrong. Open my heart to what You want me to see. Open the heart of another today so that they can see Your grace and glory.*

*In Jesus's name, I pray.*

*Amen.*

The Lord is trustworthy in all he promises and faithful in all he does. (Psalms 145:13 NIV)

## Dear Lord,

*Thank You for walking beside me, for being with me always. Your words and comfort fill me. Forgive me for times when I allow stress and worry to win my attention. I know it's OK to let go of things that are trying to demand my attention elsewhere. I will stop today and let Your Holy Spirit wash over me, fill me, and guide me.*

*Lord, let me have the personal courage to do what You ask me to do or to change what You tell me to change, to be able to put faith before pride.*

*My hope is in You, Lord.*

*In Jesus's name, I pray.*

*Amen.*

## Dear Lord,

*Glory to God! Thank You for Your blessings in my life. Thank You for the wisdom and grace You have shown me and given me.*

*Forgive me for the pride that threatens to always take over. Teach me to know I am less and You are more, to pause and turn to You. Selah. To be still and just listen to You. My pride gets in my way and makes me feel inferior at times and superior other times. Show me that being humble is where I need to be at all times. I acknowledge and admit my weaknesses and hand them to You. I will abide in You today.*

*Lord, nothing is impossible when I seek You and when I honor You. You are with me. Renew my hope every morning. Set my awareness and expectations of all that You are and all that You have to give me.*

*In Jesus's name, I pray.*

*Amen.*

## Dear Lord,

*Thank You for Your presence in my life. Thank You for choosing me and always being by me side. Forgive me for my sins today and forgive those who sin against me. I rebuke the enemy's attempts to try to distract me. Let me lead with Your love in everything I do today.*

*Give me the peace that overcomes all negativity that tries to find its way. I rebuke the negative and claim Your righteousness. I declare that I am found in You! I pick up my cross today in obedience to You as my Lord and Savior, obeying Your Word.*

*Lead me to pause and see everything through Your eyes, to shine grace in others today. Less of me and more of You. Glory to God for all that You do!*

*In Jesus's name, I pray all this.*

*Amen.*

# Dear Lord,

*Bless those I meet today. Guide me with Your words of grace and wisdom.*

*Lord, I ask that You increase and elevate my prayer life, that I may walk boldly as who You have called me to be. I ask that You help me to see through Your eyes and to want You as much as You want me. I ask You to keep Your voice clear in my head.*

*Lord, I ask that You teach me Your ways and not let me depart from them. I know I will never lose or be forsaken, for You are with me. Guide me, show me, train me. Tear down any unrighteousness motives I may have. Release any chains that bind me. Lead me to Your grace.*

*I decree and declare that I pick up my cross today and carry it to remind me of what You did for me, to remind me that all my ways should be left at the cross. Not my will but Your will be done today.*

*In Jesus's name, I pray.*

*Amen.*

## Dear Lord,

*Wash me clean today. Stir up the gifts You have placed in me so I can be successful in the spaces You have appointed me. Reveal Your glory to me and bring meaning to every mess in my life.*

*Lord, You go before me, behind me, and all around me. You walk beside me through everything in my day. Let me be aware of Your presence constantly. Thank You for being the light in the darkness. Thank You for Your wisdom and guidance. Thank You for being a God of hope! I believe by faith that it is so!*

*In Jesus's name, I pray.*

*Amen.*

## Dear Lord,

*I am so grateful for the moments I can spend with You. The refreshing feeling I receive from You each morning reminds me to strive for this during the day. Lord, forgive those who are unaware of Your presence. Forgive me when I don't turn to You during the day in times of need.*

*I will remind my soul of Your promises and put my hope in God alone. Nothing is too big or too small for You. I have so much more to do and live for each day than just what I see. Let me silence my emotions and insecurities today and quietly abide in You. Let me trust Your ways. I will remember all the times You rescued and blessed me.*

*Lord, let my hope in You be the anchor to my soul, strong and secure. Teach me to stop and fix my heart on Your Word today, on the promises You have given me. Let me be present in this season and not be impatient about tomorrow. Let me pause, selah, my soul.*

*In Jesus's name, I have faith.*

*Amen.*

# Dear Lord,

*I praise You! Let me rest in You and trust in Your grace through faith. I rest in the fact that You are my comforter and counselor. Today I will be on Your path, not my own. I know that all my faith and hope won't cause any storms to disappear, but Your strength fills the gap in my weakness. Lord, be greater than my heart. I put my hope in You, my source of all things. Be still my soul and let me realize that You are my strength in every occasion, my source of all power. Reveal in me the ways that will help me grow more ferocious in my faith. Give me Your supernatural favor and joy. Help my heart and soul to not only embrace and cling to the truth that You find me worthy of Your favor and joy, but to deeply receive it in Your name and for Your glory. Continue to move me, to push me forward with the passion that only the Holy Spirit can give. Let me complete my passion with my praises of Your goodness and creation.*

*In Jesus's name, I pray.*

*Amen.*

## Dear Lord,

*I pray You will help me change my mind if my thoughts are not aligned with Your will and Your way for my life. I pray that You will strengthen me to be greater than I was yesterday.*

*Lord, help me to apply my mind to only things that will benefit me. Help me to surrender and hold captive any thought that threatens my peace or hope in You.*

*Lord, I come against any seeds of thoughts that have been planted in my life or my mind by the enemy. I declare and decree You have full authority over me.*

*Lord, teach me when it's time to strengthen my spirit and when it's time to rest in You. Show me how to be a kingdom warrior. You are my way maker, promise keeper, and the light in any darkness!*

*In Jesus's name, I pray.*

*Amen.*

> And hope does not put us to shame, because God's love has been poured out into our hearts through the Holy Spirit, who has been given to us. (Romans 5:5 NIV)

## Dear Lord,

*I praise You for all the goodness You have given me. My life is complete with You. Lord, forgive me for impatient and desperate thoughts. Lord, I am so grateful for the time I have with You. It's so hard to leave this place. You always show me how mighty You are and how small the enemy's attacks are in comparison. In the middle of the raging and brutal storm, I know that You will come to me. I may not recognize You, but You will come for me. I just need to look up. You have promised that You will never leave me or forsake me. Teach me to be stronger when the enemy attempts to distract me or derail my faith in my circumstances. Lord, my trust is in You. Fill me with Your Holy Spirit today!*

*In Jesus's name, I pray.*

*Amen.*

# Dear Lord,

*You are the great I Am. You are the only one in control. Thank You for being our glory, our blessings, our peace in the midst of the chaos.*

*Lord, I know that the prayers we had to close all the clubs didn't happen, so we trust in You to show us what You want us to do. Thank You, Jesus, for giving us the time, the hope through You, and the love that You fill us with to show the lost and the hurting. Give us Your grace and wisdom to know what You want each of us to say.*

*Lead us on Your path and be the light that fills any darkness in Your name. Lord, I declare and decree Your love will touch lives today. Mountains will be moved for Your glory. It's by faith that we are one for Your Word.*

*Thank You, Jesus, for giving me this wonderful purpose!*

*In Jesus's name, may God bless us and protect us!*

*Amen.*

May you be blessed by the Lord, the maker of Heaven and Earth. (Psalms 115:15 NIV)

# Dear Lord,

*Glory to You, Lord. We thank You for Your blessings. With humility and surrender, I come before You. Let me be humble, not prideful, in Your presence, to look up when I'm doubtful and find my strength and my salvation. Teach me to be weak, not in this world's definition of weak but so that I know You go before me, to find the strength and richness only You provide in my weakness, surrendering my pride to find true humility and see God's magnificence.*

*Lord, remind me to bow more often, to look up more often, and to never forget Your never-ending grace and love. Fill me always with Your reliable hope in what I cannot see or control. Teach me, Lord, to not get tangled up in my own plans and executions but to place all confidence in You, that all my expectations will be fulfilled in Your timing. Remove any spirit that isn't producing fruit and give me clarity of mind and clarity of vision so I can see through Your eyes only.*

*I pray this in Jesus's name.*

*Amen.*

# Dear Lord,

*Forgive anything that is a hindrance to my prayers today. Open my heart to see and feel Your presence.*

*Lord, fill me with Your peace, strength, and joy overflowing so I may be hope to others.*

*Let my prayers be bold and intentional, asking for things that are way out of my control and reach. I know that Your royal blood flows through me because I am Your daughter. I feel You with me always. On the highest mountain or the lowest valley, You are always with me. You are my refuge when I need peace and my cheerleader and encourager of all things good and beautiful.*

*Lord, I know Your plans for me are greater than those I can see. Give me the treasures of knowledge, scripture, and the Holy Spirit. Let me use them to discover the depth and blessedness that abounds from hope.*

*In Jesus's name, I pray.*

*Amen.*

# Dear Lord,

I know You made me to always remember You, to not forget You. Yet sometimes I don't ask for Your wisdom in decisions during my day. You gave me an independent mind that can still be influenced by the world around me. What I see, hear, and feel aren't the right influences. The world influences me and gives me choices on how to live in it that don't agree with Your path for me.

Lord, You gave me a heart that wants to love and give hope to others, not to be distracted by other things, not to pull away from You. When I'm not turned to You, my thoughts aren't aligned with Yours. Lord, I want to learn more. I want to desire more than what is physically in front of me. I want to be taken deeper spiritually, not by humankind but by You. Lord, let me stop trying to solve everything and worrying about things I can't control. Let me turn more toward You instead. Pursue me. I surrender my heart to You. Clear my head and cleanse my heart so I know what Your love is.

In Jesus's name, I pray.

Amen.

## Dear Lord,

*You are my rock and my foundation. I know I need to stop questioning myself and my life because I'm actually questioning You about Your plans for me. I'm questioning my trust in You, Lord. You tell me to look up and know.*

*Lord, empty my heart of all things that aren't You. Fill my heart with only Your goodness. Take away all my frustrations. Take away any self-pity, stress, anxiety, and feelings of being out of control and throw them in the ocean to dissolve into tiny grains of sand. Lord, I don't want to be selfish, greedy, proud, or envious. I don't want to judge others. Release in me the desire to be closer to You, to be more like You. Let me drop all my worries at Your feet and pick up my cross to remind me of who I am and what I should do each day. Remind me I'm not in control, that You protect me. Lord, open my eyes so I'm not blind to Your path. Open my ears so I can hear Your whispers, trusting You deeper than I have before. I know You are with me, and I know You are for me.*

*I declare and decree You will always be with me. I confess my fear of letting go of the control I think I have.*

*In Jesus's name, I pray.*

*Amen.*

In his unfailing love, my God will stand with me. He will let me look down in triumph on all my enemies. (Psalms 59:10 NLT)

# Dear Lord,

*Begin again in me. Give me fresh, new eyes to see. You know me. You know where I'm going. I know I don't need to prove myself to You because You have me, and that's enough for You.*

*Let me pause so I can be with You, so I can see You before me, so I can listen to Your messages telling me I am loved, I am powerful, I am hope, I am Your beloved daughter.*

*Hold my thoughts, my dreams, my fears. Contain them and gather them up in Your strong hands so they will never crush me.*

*Place Your hand on my heart and seek my soul and spirit so I can always be connected to You. Fill me always with songs of praise so I never stop praising and rejoicing in You.*

*Lord, keep me in Your peace and rebuke the whispers that try to call me away from the truth.*

*Be still my soul and fill my heart with only Your truth. Your truth is my armor. Your words are the light in the darkness. They feed me and nourish me. Your words make me new again.*

*In Jesus Christ's powerful name.*

*Amen.*

## Dear Lord,

*Fill up this place where You've planted me. I want the everlasting peace that only You give. I want Your hand upon my heart. Hear what my heart says and fix it so I only want You. Nothing else will come first.*

*Remind me how deep Your love is for me. In the middle of a hectic day, stop me to pause and breathe You in. You are my strength and the energy I desire. You are healing and restoration. Let me lift up my eyes and see You. Focusing on You, Lord, let me see with Your eyes and Your heart. Nourish me.*

*I will take Your hand so You can guide me today on the path that You created for me, to persevere and produce Your fruit.*

*Thank You, Jesus, for all the blessings You have given me, the easy ones and the tough ones.*

*In Jesus's name, I pray.*

*Amen.*

We have this hope as an anchor for the soul, firm and secure. It enters the inner sanctuary behind the curtain. (Hebrews 6:19 NIV)

## Dear Lord,

*Let me stay right here with You, with all Your glory, and praise You. You fill my whole being with hope and love. Every deep breath I take will slow my pace and push the uncontrollable chaos away. Your unconditional love pours over me and into me. Let me accept it and not push it away. Show me the things You want me to see, through Your eyes. Put Your song in my heart that only my ears can hear and recognize as You. Let me rebuke all the fast-paced drama around me. Let me release the pride that threatens to take over when I am at peace. I surrender, Lord, to everything You have for me. Remind me to pause and selah. Hold my hand, and I will know You.*

*In Jesus's name, I pray.*

*Amen.*

## Dear Lord,

*I declare that You are always with me. I have nothing to fear. I open and humble my heart and feel every fear and anxiety float out and away on the wind. You are bigger than every thought, every ache, and every fear. You stand before me in the gap between belief and unbelief. You stand before me, my Lord, as my rescuer, my redeemer. You stand before me, and I know I am not forgotten. I know I am held, and I won't let go.*

*Lord, I ask for and want more of You in my life. I ask You to come deeper into my life. Show me deeper joy and deeper freedom so that when this world is throwing darts to destroy, I can stand on the fact that none of it will harm me. Lord, You know me. I trust You. I know You are with me. I know You will love me and guide me and protect me from myself. Remind me to rest, open my heart, and let go.*

*In Jesus's name, I pray, and to Him all the glory!*

*Amen.*

Pour out all your worries and stress upon him and leave them there, for he always tenderly cares for you. (1 Peter 5:7 TPT)

## Dear Lord,

*I give You all my life, all my love. Show me the gift You have in me. Teach me how to use that gift, to not feel I have to prove something but to be at peace.*

*I want to give what You give me, to receive love from love, and to give love. Let that be my reaction. Help me truly accept Your love, all of it, so I do not accept things from my past as my outcome, my end.*

*Deliver my heart and soul to the place that can see, hear, and feel Your love always.*

*Lord, I worship You. You are the one who redeemed me and restored me. No other person or thing has done that for me.*

*Lord, give me the faith to be stronger in Your will, never doubting Your gifts or letting life and unknowns get in the way. Abide in me, Lord, forever.*

*In Jesus's name, I pray.*

*Amen.*

## Dear Lord,

*You are so faithful. Remind me every morning to let go of the chase, to turn toward You and grasp Your hand.*

*Remind me not to panic in the moments when things and circumstances aren't perfect but to open my eyes and see You standing in the middle of the storm.*

*Lord, I let go of all idols that try to control me and my thoughts. I will love You first today. I will turn to You first today. I will see only You.*

*Teach me to focus on only the positives in every situation. Teach me how to move forward and to continue to lay down the idols and circumstances that make me stumble, to seek validation only from You.*

*Search my heart and reveal what doesn't give me peace, what is standing in my way to be closer to You.*

*Lord, You are my rock, and I stand firm in You!*

*In Jesus's name, I pray.*

*Amen.*

## Dear Lord,

*Forgive me for my sins. I turn them all over to You. Lord, let me forgive those who have sinned against me.*

*Let me embrace hope on purpose, so it influences my thoughts, my attitude, and my outlook today. Let it release the joy that is my strength. Help me to be expectant of Your good things and to remember that You are always looking to be good to me. Renew my hope today and help me to declare Your victory through my thoughts and actions.*

*Lord, give me the kind of peace that cannot be given by anyone or anything but You. Let me stand firm in that peace and know that Your grace surrounds me, no matter what. Work Your desires into my heart and then fulfill those desires as Your will, not mine. Let others see not just me but instead know and perceive Your stronger presence.*

*In Jesus's name, I pray!*

*Amen.*

# Dear Lord,

*Praise and all glory to You! Thank You for all the blessings You have given me in my life, for the grace You have shown me and Your never-ending love for me. Forgive me when my mind runs away with thoughts inconsistent with You and Your plan for me.*

*Lord, bless me with Your strength and shelter today. Show me what others need. Break my heart as theirs are broken. Fill this void of brokenness with the love that only You give. Holy Spirit, guide me with Your truth. Your worthiness fills me.*

*Lord, bless my family, both close and far, direct and extended. I hold firmly to the confidence and hope of my relationship in You. Let me take every opportunity today to show others You in me.*

*In Jesus's name, I pray.*

*Amen.*

> Now faith is confidence in what we hope for and assurance about what we do not see. (Hebrews 11:1 NIV)

## Dear Lord,

*I praise You for all the goodness, all the love that You give me. Lord, Yours is the glory for all that is.*

*Lord, forgive me for my sins and forgive those who will sin against me. Open their eyes to Your love and mercy. Lord, let me be open to always building on the strengths You have made in me, to know and accept that You are always in control, to know and accept that I'm not You and I don't have to do it all to please You. Let me be curious and vulnerable to You, to be humble with the blessings You give me. It's all for Your glory on Your timetable, not mine.*

*Lord, let me always be obedient to You. Let me be the love that seeks to please the object that You desire.*

*In Jesus's name, I pray.*

*Amen.*

## Dear Lord,

Thank You for this beautiful day, for all the blessings You have given and will give me today. Lord, let me know Your heart today. Show me what I should know today and accept it with Your grace and an open heart.

Lord, speak to me by Your spirit, Your written Word, and the assurance of Your direction.

Open my heart to know when You speak to me and want me to take action or be still. Don't let my pride take over, making me unable to soak up Your Word. Fill me with the spirit and wisdom to move forward in Your name. Forgive me of any thoughts that are counterproductive to Your purpose for me. And let me love others in only the capacity and ways that are in Your image.

In Jesus's name, I pray.

Amen.

> May the God of hope fill you with all joy and peace as you trust in him, so that you may overflow with hope by the power of the Holy Spirit. (Romans 15:13 NIV)

# Dear Lord,

*Thank You for being my rock and foundation, for guiding me when I am lost. Show me today what You want me to see. Mold in me what You want me to feel. Show me how to pray as easily as I breathe.*

*Lord, forgive me for trying to make decisions without You.*

*Let me submit to Your ways, to produce only the fruit of the spirit. Empty me from all my selfish thoughts and fill me with the strong and good will of Jesus Christ. It's only through You that all things are possible.*

*In Jesus's name, I pray.*

*Amen.*

# Dear Lord,

*I praise You! You brought me out of darkness into light. Slowly but surely, the lessons and experiences that I thought were for my fate, You used for my good. You gave me the choice of continued darkness or light that was warm, full of life, peaceful, joyful.*

*Lord, You have given me life abundantly. You came to set the captives free of all the enemy' lies. I declare and decree that every chain in my life is broken. I am free from all the lies. The kingdom of darkness has no power on me. The enemy will not succeed, because, Jesus, You have triumphed! You are victorious! I claim that victory from today onward.*

*In Jesus's name, I pray.*

*Amen.*

Be joyful in hope, patient in affliction faithful in prayer. (Romans 12:12 NIV)

# Dear Lord,

*Please bless and forgive Your children from our sins. Your love is powerful and can compel each of us to walk into Your light and abandon the darkness. Lord, we know that no human love can ever match Yours. Yet we still don't believe it.*

*Lord, fill me with Your boundless love. Let me know You and Your unmeasurable love. Only Your love can create the true emotions of the Spirit that reside in me. Lord, awaken the Spirit in each of us. The sun will always rise and overcome the darkness. Give us the determination in Your name to believe this.*

*Soften and open each of our hearts, Lord. Mend the broken hearts with Your never-denying love. Let me sense, see, and hear Your Spirit that always comforts me and be that reflection to others.*

*In Jesus's blessed name, I pray.*

*Amen.*

# Dear Lord,

*I praise You! I keep You in my heart always! Thank You for all the blessings and glory in my life. To You alone is all the glory.*

*Lord, for the woman who needs to feel Your love today, please give her eyes to see and ears to hear Your love for her. You know her name, her triumphs, her past, and her wounds. Let her know it is never too late to call on You. Anything she has ever done or experienced is already covered by Your blood and Your sacrifice. It is never too late to ask for Your forgiveness, to give her life for Your service, to rebuke and deny the enemy that entangles her and live free in You. Lord, for those alone or feeling unloved, let their love for You be so fierce that it radiates back to them. Let them live each day knowing You love them more than they can imagine and that they are not alone.*

*In Jesus's name, I pray.*

*Amen.*

## Dear Lord,

*Thank You for this day, for the blessings You have given me. Forgive me of my sins today, for any negative thinking that would condemn others. Lord, please forgive those who sin against us. They are not in Christ yet, so they don't understand what they are doing or why. I know that is not You but the enemy that is trying to worm his way in. You are only the good that surrounds us. Lord, search my heart and send me the name of the one You want me to help. I know You take all that is ugly, dirty, and shameful away. In its place, You put with Your kingdom's purpose, because everything that happens when our hearts are broken is used for our good. Lord, help me to remember every day that we are all equal to Your grace. Let us realize our own spiritual bankruptcy so we can see others and be humble to them.*

*Lord, Your direction for me today is to be courageous and humble in Your name, to lift up the one You have put on my heart. In Jesus's name, I receive it and obey Your will.*

*Amen.*

As for me, I will always have hope; I will praise you more and more. (Psalm 71:14 NIV)

# Dear Lord,

Thank You for this beautiful day! Let us be fruitful and deliver Your Word through the Holy Spirit to someone who needs it, someone You put in front of us today.

Lord, tenderize my heart as I pray for my enemies. Bless those who have mocked me, those who offend me, and those who curse me. Give me the compassion of Jesus as I lift them before Your throne.

Thank You, Jesus, for being my ultimate provider, for meeting all my needs with Your rich glory. I yield myself to a life of bold and believing prayer. I trust You with my present and my future. Surround the unspoken with Your angel armies to defend and protect them. Shine Your light so brightly it blinds the enemy. Fix the eyes and emotions of our hearts solely on You. Let us be Your embers to ignite the fire in the one.

In Jesus Christ's name, I pray.

Amen.

# Dear Lord,

*Forgive me for my thoughts of despair or doubt. Plant in my heart the strength and knowledge that You are in control, the strength to stand firm in You.*

*Let me let go of any anxiety or stress that threatens to rob me of Your peace and joy.*

*Lord, I know it is and always will be Your will and not mine. Nothing can harm me when I let go of the control and deliver it to You. You have me in a Your strong right hand.*

*Make me strong in the knowledge that Your mercy and grace will defeat anything. I just need to believe in You and love You. Help me to see and feel Your presence in what I do and who I meet today. Fill me with Your Holy Spirit so that I overflow with Your fruit. Empty me of anything that tries to steal my good thoughts away.*

*Lord, You are so good and so gracious to me. I know in my heart I am Your child, and Your mercy, love, and grace are great toward me!*

*In Jesus's name, I pray all this to be true!*

*Amen.*

# Dear Lord,

*Thank You for Your Spirit that dwells in me!*

*Release the revelation of Your glory spirit. Release the revelation realm of God's glory through me today. Use me today in the gifts that only the Holy Spirit discerns.*

*Lord, strengthen me by touching my mind, emotions, and speech with Your presence. Let me see You at work.*

*Lord, give me wisdom for every area of my life and take any pride away. Show me how to walk with You in intimate love steps. Don't let my eyes' focus and direction leave Your face.*

*And, Lord, I know You came on a rescue mission to seek and save the lost. Let me be Your hands and feet through Your Holy Spirit to faithfully seek and help the one who is lost. You know their name. Introduce me to them.*

*In Jesus's name, I pray.*

*Amen.*

## Dear Lord,

*It is through Your amazing grace and incredible love that I am who I am, saved by grace and all my sins forgiven through my faith in You. Lord, I lift my heart in humble thanks for the glories of Your grace. Thank You that we don't have to earn a drop of the mighty river of grace that flows freely to each of us daily. Thank You for the unmerited and unexpected favor You shower on my life. Help me not to ever forget my discipline to turn to You and drink from Your water of life. I am nothing without You in my life. Thank You, Jesus, for all that You give me. I surrender.*

*In Jesus's name, I pray.*

*Amen.*

# Dear Lord,

*Forgive me of my sins and judging thoughts. Forgive those who judge against me. Lord, bless my enemies with Your grace and favor.*

*Lord, show me what my heart holds close. Reveal it so I can leave it at the cross—anything impure. Let nothing come from mouth today that is not words of encouragement and hope to others. Let the words be echoes of what's in my heart. Lord, give me strength to let go of things I either don't agree with or don't understand. It's not for me to judge. Bring strength of grace and mercy to these thoughts and defeat them. Lord, build up Your presence in my life today so that I may be more humble and loving to others, trusting only in Your Word through the Holy Spirit in me and through the faithfulness I choose.*

*In Jesus's name, I pray.*

*Amen.*

# Dear Lord,

*Thank You for Your never-ending mercy. Thank You for the love You surround me with. Lord, please forgive me of any sins, any thoughts that are self-defeating. Lord, forgive me for always trying to go without You. Don't let me judge this day by its difficulties but by the Joy You bring to me. Let me have the continuous faith I need today to make any problem-solving secondary to the true goal of living closer to You. I surrender to You, Lord.*

*Lord, give me a heart that is worthy of You today. Open my heart so I obey Your Word and truly love as You have loved me. Show me how to be bold and stand in Your name. Teach me every day so I can be more like You.*

*In Jesus's name, I pray.*

*Amen.*

## Dear Lord,

*Thank You for Your glory, blessings, and true love! Forgive me for when I have thoughts of doubt or worry. I know that's when I'm furthest away from You. You are my provider and protector through every day. I rest in the knowledge that I am complete in You. I choose to trust You and not doubt You in my circumstances. Because You are with me, everything that happens in my day will be used for my good.*

*I am willing to follow You, Jesus, through every valley and mountaintop You take me. I affirm Your goodness in me.*

*In Jesus Christ's name, I pray.*

*Amen.*

# Dear Lord,

*Thank You for being good and just. I am grateful.*

*Forgive me for all the doubt I have, for the many thoughts of busyness and injustice. What do I have to compare that to anyway?*

*I know Your timing is not my timing, and my focus should be on today—to be in the right here, right now and not worry about tomorrow.*

*Let me focus on faith and hope each moment of every day.*

*Lord, whet my appetite to want to know You more. Change the desires of my heart to better line up to Your heart. Open my heart to receive Your overflowing love—to know, really know, it's for me. Help me to seek and have faith, not perfection.*

*Keep me from being concerned with what others think of me and help me turn away from that form of idolatry. Let me rest in Your loving arms and truly receive Your deep peace. Lord, I worship You in spirit and faith so that I can shine as a brilliant testimony to Your presence and power in my life.*

*In Jesus's name, I pray.*

*Amen.*

## Dear Lord,

*I praise You for all Your blessings and mercies. You have shown me Your grace and Your miracles constantly. Lord, I am grateful! In Your abundance, You deliver more than what I see.*

*Lord, no matter the circumstances, I seek Your safety and security always.*

*Lord, please guide those around us with discernment and wisdom to lay down their burdens at Your feet and be at peace.*

*Through You, all things are possible. You are the great I Am, the Alpha and the Omega. Nothing happens without Your hands!*

*In Jesus's name, I trust and pray this!*

*Amen.*

# Dear Lord,

*Thank You for Your strength, for Your arms that hold me, for Your Holy Spirit that fills me in my time of need. Lord, please forgive my doubts and daily distractions. I know Your peace is given to me daily—peace for the present so I don't get ahead of myself. I am content to live with the mystery and to follow You. May I always rely on You. I will always approach Your throne of grace with the confidence to receive Your peace with a thankful heart.*

*Let me yield my heart to Your grace and wisdom to do whatever You ask. Do not let my emotions dictate my thoughts, my thoughts dictate my decisions, my decisions determine my behavior, or my behavior decide my relationships. Let me be whole in You only, so that my faith in Your Word is all I rely on.*

*In Jesus's name, I pray.*

*Amen.*

# Dear Lord,

*Thank You for Your presence daily, for Your roots that run deep in me. I know that every minute of every day, You are with me.*

*Lord, please forgive me for my doubts and worrying about things I have no control over. Let me do what's possible and release the rest into Your hands. My worries are just distortions of my reality, not my instinct or my intuition. Release me from the chains that cycle my worries through my head. I replace them with praise to You. Help me to capture the spiraling thoughts and bring peace to the mental chaos. I am no longer a slave to my emotions or my circumstances. I am aware of the power that lives deep in me. I am equipped to fight on the front lines of the battlefield of my thoughts. I am equipped for this battle that tells me who I am and who You are. Help me to never be a victim to my thoughts and to remember I am not a victim because You are already victorious.*

*Lord, it's in Your name, Jesus Christ, that I pray.*

*Amen.*

## Dear Lord,

*Open my eyes so I can see all that You have given me to disarm and defeat the enemy. Give me strength to lay down everything at Your feet, to submit to You and pick up my cross. Be still my soul. Lord, I want You and Your truths to reign in my mind. I believe in Your name and the right to be a child of God and share in Your glory.*

*In Jesus's name, I pray.*

Amen.

## Dear Lord,

*I praise Your goodness and mercy. Please give me peace of mind and calm my anxious heart. Be still my soul when I can't find my balance, when I worry about things out of my control. Shift my thoughts out of the negative, crazy, spiraling thoughts and teach me to practice taking them captive and practice the never-ending faith in You. Help the focus to be solely on You.*

*Give me the strength and clarity of mind to walk only on the path You have laid out for me.*

*I trust Your love, God, and I know You heal all stress, just as the sun will rise each day to block out the darkness. Let my eyes see the light in every moment, the light that is You.*

*In Jesus's name, I pray.*

*Amen.*

## Dear Lord,

*I choose today to take every thought captive because I know that You are more powerful than my thoughts, my circumstances, or any fears that threaten me.*

*I know that I can stand firm and trust Your process because the benefits of doing so will far outweigh what I can see. The enemy cannot distract me because I am eternally secure in You. I declare the Gospel fearlessly! Thank You, Jesus!*

*In Jesus's name, I pray.*

*Amen.*

*Your sun will never set again ... the Lord will be your everlasting light. (Isaiah 60:20 NIV)*

# Dear Lord,

*Thank You! I am so grateful for all the blessings You've given and shown me.*

*Lord, forgive me for not obeying Your early-morning call. I know You are testing my obedience, but I still go back to sleep. Lord, release that stronghold on me.*

*Lord, let me display the peace that transcends circumstances, so I can feel Your peace in the middle of the chaos. I trust Your goodness and mercy.*

*I know I can't always figure it out, but I can bring it to You because You are always available to me if I seek You.*

*Let me search for Your direction and guidance in everything so that only You lead my responses and actions.*

*Show me that there is positive in everything You lead me to do. I will let You fight my battles, but I will always suit up to protect and defend against the enemy's attempts to sidetrack me. I lay my burdens, my fear, and worries at Your feet.*

*In the name of Jesus Christ, I pray.*

*Amen.*

# Dear Lord,

*Thank You, Lord, for all Your blessings in my life, from the safety You give me to the peace I feel with You.*

*I know Your strength is like the oceans, deep and powerful and never-ending, but at the same time, You are peaceful and constant like the sound of the waves when they lap the shores.*

*Lord, I crucify my flesh and surrender to Your will. I trust in You and hold my peace close. My foundation is in You, the peace that transcends every situation, the peace that only the Holy Spirit can deliver, peace that is active and a confident trust, no matter what's going on around me.*

*I stand firm in Your light. You guide me, mature me, and strengthen me in my weakness. Forgive the sins I've committed and forgive those who sin against me. Expose the area in my heart that lacks peace, so I can grow in Your wisdom.*

*Lord, lead my thoughts, my actions, and my heart today. Your guided restraint and self-control will lead my pathway and my steps.*

*In Jesus's name, I pray.*

*Amen.*

> Hope deferred makes the heart sick, but a longing fulfilled is a tree of life. (Proverbs 13:12 NIV)

## Dear Lord,

I will suit up today in Your armor that protects me and guides me.
I put on my helmet of salvation to protect my thoughts and to remind me
to take every thought captive, to counter with Your Word, Your truth.
I will not fear, for You are with me.
I put on my belt of truth. Nothing but the truth of Your promises will do
today.
I will not fear, for You are with me.
I put on my breastplate of righteousness and stand firm and tall. I am a
child of God with royal blood flowing through me.
I will not fear, for You are with me.
I put on my shoes that are the gospel of peace. Everywhere I go today, I will
take that peace with me. I will share that peace with the one.
I will not fear, for You are with me.
I pick up my sword of the Spirit. The Holy Spirit guides me and speaks to
me. I just need to listen. I will listen for His soft whispers that will fill me
and guide me.
I will not fear, for You are with me.
Lastly, I will pick up my shield of faith, the faith that comes from knowing
You. I know that my shield protects me from any attempts from the enemy.
I know that You always go before me. You are behind me, and Your angel
armies surround me.
I will not fear, for You are with me!
Thank You, Lord, for all my blessings that have gotten me to
this place.
To You all the glory!
In Jesus's name, I pray.
Amen.

## Dear Lord,

*Forgive me of my sins today. Open my heart and reveal to me what is hidden inside. Lord, give me strength and discipline to listen to You, to obey Your Word always. Lord, let my body be a sacrifice to You and let my mind and heart always worship You in truth and spirit. Lord, let the Holy Spirit guide my thoughts and my words. Help them be used for good. Lord, guide my steps and my mouth to always proclaim Your name in glory and praise.*

*I declare that Your angel armies are protecting the weak and scared. That they can find strength and hope in You.*

*In Jesus's name, I pray.*

*Amen.*

The Lord is my strength and my shield; my heart trusts in him, and he helps me. (Psalms 28:7 NIV)

# Dear Lord,

Whether intentional or not, let there be forgiveness from my heart, not just from my lips.

Lord, search my heart. Uncover what is hiding in my heart so that I can be aware of it, so I can give it up and hand it over to You.

Lord, I know there are so many things that I have no control over. It's my will that I need to control. Give me the strength and faithfulness to hand over these things to You. Lord, help me to listen to You and to see You when You want to show me, to be patient and wait when Your answer doesn't come right away or when the solution isn't clear. Show me the steps You want me to take. I will take them

In Your name and for Your glory. Slow me down to receive all that You have for me, no matter how small.

In Jesus's name, I pray.

Amen.

## Dear Lord,

*I pray this morning that I follow Your will today, that I don't get distracted by things that are out of my control or what the enemy tries to tell me, but I focus only on what the Holy Spirit tells me.*

*Lord, I forgive those who may sin against me, and I ask for Your forgiveness for my sins.*

*Lead me, Lord. Open my heart to Your love. Open my eyes to what's in front of me, not way down the road and not the darkness that the enemy tries to put there but the truth. Open my mind to Your words confidently so that my praise is hopeful and faithful.*

*Lord, give me wisdom today to understand Your messages and Your will. I don't always understand it, but I know it's the way. Guard me against the enemy and his attempts to make me feel less than. I know I was made in Your image and Your plans for me are good and full.*

*In Jesus's glorious name, I pray.*

*Amen.*

## Dear Lord,

*Forgive me for the shame that I bring to You.*

*Lord, I know that when I seek You with all my heart, You are there for me. You are here this morning showing me Your love. You show me Your mercy and grace. Even though I am blind with impatience, You gave me Your message and love. You put Your arms around me to be still and listen to You. Your power is strong in the right here, right now when we ask with all of ourselves, not trying to be perfect, just coming to You as we are. I know You have a plan for me that is good. And I know it's one day by one day.*

*Lord, I seek You with my whole heart. I am on my knees at Your feet and submit to Your will. I hear You and promise to always obey You, even when it's not comfortable. Your plans are greater than mine could ever be. Lord, let me be still and experience You and see You working. Open my eyes to see You, not this world. I trust that You are always doing what's best for me.*

*In Jesus's name, I pray in love and faith.*

*Amen.*

## Dear Lord,

*Deliver me, Lord, from my enemies and show me Your love. I have hope in Your justice, and I know You can defeat them and deliver me from the enemy that tries to destroy those I love. I know that You, Lord, and only You can defeat them.*

*Thank You, Lord, for Your goodness and the strength You give me. With You, nothing can come against me. You will fight those battles for me.*

*Lord, You go before me, and You are the light in my darkness. I am faithful of Your deliverance and righteousness. I will not turn from You, but I will fix my eyes on You. My strength and my hope come from You. Thank You, Jesus.*

*In Jesus's name, I pray.*

*Amen.*

## Dear Lord,

*With You, there is no darkness. You are pure and good.*

*Bring Your light and restore Your presence to the dark places. Let us bring Your hope to the hearts that feel defeated. Bring Your love and compassion to those in pain. Shine Your light of hope in the darkness of this world. Help me take moments to be still and sit and feel Your presence, releasing all the worries I have to You. You are trustworthy, good, and loving. Let me stand in Your armor. Give me Your light and pour the blood of Jesus on each of Your warriors.*

*In Jesus's name.*

*Amen.*

## Dear Lord,

*You always go before me. You fight my battles for me and right all the wrongs. Let me be patient and wait for You instead of charging ahead myself.*

*Lord, search my heart and show me where there are shadows. Show me so light can expose them. Lord, teach me to not be prideful but only humble in Your name.*

*You are my light. You have chosen me to be Your light in the darkness. Holy Spirit, be with me today so the words that come out of my mouth and the thoughts in my head are only Yours. Fix my eyes to see those who are the last, the least, and the lost. To those who have embraced fear and doubt, show them*

*Your light through me. For all those I meet today who need to see Your love, let me have Your grace to be Your servant and give them Your hope and love in that darkness.*

*Thank You for shining Your light through me.*

*In Jesus's name.*

*Amen.*

> But those who hope in the Lord will renew their strength. They will soar on wings like eagles; they will run and not grow weary, they will walk and not be faint. (Isaiah 40:31 NIV)

## Dear Lord,

*Forgive me, Father, for the sins of my heart and mind. Let me forgive others who have sinned against me. Search my heart and show me what I need to see. What am I missing? What am I not seeing because my pride gets in the way? Wash me clean from what it is with the blood of Jesus.*

*Lord, I know I can't control anything and that You are making my path straight, but my pride always gets in the way, and I think I know better. Letting go of the wheel is so very hard for me. Whether it's old hurt feelings or figuring out how to do my job better, I always forget to just let it go. When I do, the experience You show me is so much better. If I can just lay it at Your feet. Forgive me. I want to obey and trust You, Lord.*

*Please show me Your grace and guide me on Your path of righteousness. I have no room in this life for the enemy's schemes. Show me how to love everyone and all circumstances, unconditionally and truly with all my heart.*

*In Jesus's name, I pray.*

*Amen.*

# Dear Lord,

*Forgive me for my sins and forgive those who will and have sinned against me. Lord, let me live by the Spirit, not by the flesh. Give me Your grace to live each day in the control and power of the Holy Spirit. I need Your strength in me every day to avoid those quick, knee-jerk reactions to the things that happen around me.*

*Lord, grant me peace. Teach me to be quiet and thoughtful, to reach inside and allow the Holy Spirit to speak louder. Less of me and more of You.*

*Search my heart, Lord, and show me my weaknesses. Let me put to death those weaknesses and thoughts that try to mislead me.*

*In Jesus's name, I pray.*

*Amen.*

## Dear Lord,

Help me love unconditionally, to forgive others and not judge them. Help me be patient with humility and gentleness. Show me the patience I should have with love. Only through Your Holy Spirit can I be patient, with Your grace and mercy. Help me to see others the way You see them, even when they are different in the way they think, in all circumstances. Show me how to respond with compassion and kindness, even if someone is doing wrong. Let me understand that it has nothing to do with me and that a negative response from me is not worthy of Your love. Free me from the compulsion to judge so quickly. It's not my way that matters but always Your way that matters most.

In Jesus's name, I pray.

Amen.

# Dear Lord,

*Forgive me for my sins, my weakness of being fearful of the unknown. I want to experience You. I want to see You working through my life. I know that this means I will face a daily crisis of belief. I know I must trust You to be who You say You are and that You will do what You say You will do. I must continue to adjust my life to You and Your will. I will obey You, Lord. Work through me to accomplish all that You desire to accomplish. Do not let me give in to any unpromising circumstances when You are speaking to me. Do not let me be impatient. Show me where I am disobedient to Your Word. Help me to trust that You are always doing what is best for me. Give me patience to let You prepare me for the task You have assigned me. Place the Holy Spirit in me and in my life to direct my steps according to Your ways, Your purposes, and Your work. Make our relationship even closer. Show me how to love unconditionally and without limits. Thank You, Lord, for being my protector and provider. I surrender.*

*In Jesus's name, I pray.*

*Amen.*

## Dear Lord,

*Show me the truth through Your grace, the truth of who You are and what Your plans are for me. Lord, I ask for Your wisdom. Show me how to be patient and to always turn to You for the wisdom I need to navigate my day.*

*Lord, thank You for all Your mercies. Show me how the suffering we experience will lead us to perseverance. The wisdom You give me will build my character to better see through Your eyes. Build my wisdom through my faith and hope in You, Jesus.*

*In Jesus Christ's name, I pray.*

*Amen.*

## Dear Lord,

*Lord, open my heart today to be filled with Your Holy Spirit. Let Him guide my words and thoughts all for Your glory. Open my heart to truly see the obstacles and idols that I have placed there in front of You. Give me the strength and wisdom through Your righteousness and blessings to remove them, to rebuke them, to walk toward Your want for me and not my want. Let me see that mine is controlling the wrong outcome.*

*Lord, fill me with humbleness to accept Your will in my life. Empty my mind of all thoughts of control and outcome so that I will trust in Your way always.*

*Lord, this morning, I put on Your armor to protect me.*

*In Jesus's name, I declare You are my Savior.*

*Amen.*

> We wait in hope for the Lord; he is our help and our shield. (Psalm 33:20 NIV)

## Dear Lord,

Lord, teach me to let go of things that spin around me, demanding my attention. Teach me to submit to You, Lord. You are my truth. In everything I do, I submit to You. Show me what truth about You I need to experience. Show me what sins are preventing me from that truth. Lord, please show Your love through me, not frustration that always wants to be front and center. I know my way with You will be long, intentional, and deliberate. Teach me that I can't have it all, all the time, when I think I should, to learn lessons in the moment, to listen and submit to You. Show me I can't control everything. Even when I think I'm doing good, I should stop and make sure my heart is in the right place. Help me to stop where I am, to breathe and be at peace in the chaos today.

I've seen Your work, Your miracles, and Your truth, and I know You have never left me.

Walk with me today and help me be better.

In Jesus's name, I pray.

Amen.

## Dear Lord,

*Show me Your direction for my life. Give me the strength and wisdom to walk in faith, the faith that comes from Your Holy Spirit.*

*Lord, I know everything is in Your hands. All things are in Your control. Why do I always try to take over? I try to plan and create without Your direction, plans that You already have for us. Lord, thank You for Your grace and mercy, which remind me every morning to let go and have faith in You, to fix my eyes only on You and not on the many daily distractions, to stop questioning things that don't make sense, to accept them.*

*Lord, I praise You for all the blessings You have given me and for those blessings yet to come.*

*In Your name, I pray.*

## Dear Lord,

*Forgive me and stop me from reacting with frustration when things don't go exactly as I plan them. Help me see the bigger picture. Help me when I am weak in reacting by giving me patience and wisdom.*

*Lord, it's so easy and automatic to want to control things around me, to let the fear of the unknown, the quiet take over. But that's never the right answer when I can turn to You in those times.*

*Lord, let me hand everything over today, not think or worry about tomorrow but walk patiently next to You, at Your pace, not mine.*

*Lord, let me enjoy today and all its wonderful blessings as if it was my last.*

*In Jesus's name, I pray.*

*Amen.*

> May God our Father ... and the Lord Jesus Christ
> give you grace and peace. (2 Corinthians 1:2 NLT)

## Dear Lord,

*Forgive me for my sins today, the doubt and fear that try to threaten my day.*

*Let Your wisdom and kindness prevail in me, not the pride and fear that create anxiety. I pray to be less of me and more of You.*

*Lord, fill me with the knowledge of Your will for my life through the Holy Spirit, who gives me spiritual wisdom and understanding.*

*Lord, release me from the anxiety and control that try to take over constantly. Instead, fill me with Your Holy Spirit so I can immediately bring it all to You. Your Word restores the confidence in my heart that You alone have the ability to transform my heart and life!*

*Lord, I hold firmly and confidently to the hope and grace that are found in You, through Your Son, Jesus Christ.*

*In Jesus's name, I pray.*

*Amen.*

## Dear Lord,

*Forgive me for second-guessing Your true plans for my life, for trying to determine my outcome. The faith that I have comes from the power and strength that You have given me and my life. Thank You for all the blessings You show me every day.*

*Lord, sometimes I want to run ahead and create my own ending, because fear tries to control the situation. All I should do is just cling to You and Your Word. You have always shown me Your grace when I couldn't see anything. Open my eyes to just see You, Lord, to take a breath today and step back into Your grace. Open my ears so that I can hear You when You tell me what to do. Lord, give me Your patience and wisdom to sit at Your feet and wait. I know that Your ways are so much better than mine. I do not need to fear the unknown. Fear is not what You give us. Help me to know in my heart, every moment of every day and in every circumstance, that You are in control. All You ask is for me to do my very best for Your glory. I just need to be faithful to You.*

*In Jesus's name, I pray.*

*Amen.*

## Dear Lord,

*Forgive me for the sin of doubting who You are, thinking that I can do without You.*

*I know that everything You do for me is good. Somehow, I listen and sometimes believe what the enemy says to me. I rebuke all of what he says to me, right here, right now! To have him try so hard to break my focus on You confirms that I am on the right path.*

*I will continue to seek You. Your blessings on my life have been proof of Your love for me.*

*Lord, I seek You, to be closer to You and to not lose focus on what You have asked me to do.*

*Right here is where I am. Right here is where You want me to be. Teach me to be here every moment, to find the good in that moment, and to learn from You what You are teaching me. I will rise to hear You and obey You.*

*In Jesus's name, I pray.*

*Amen.*

## Dear Lord,

*Give me the wisdom to understand and identify when grace and mercy should follow the sin, rather than judgment.*

*Lord, let the hearts of those around me be opened to see what they need from You. Let me be Your hands and feet to deliver hope for those in need.*

*Lord, let me slow down in my day and be more intentional to Your Word rather than quickly reacting. Lord, let me have the faith to keep believing that You are at work in our lives, even though I might not see.*

*Lord, I ask for and receive the presence of Your Holy Spirit in me throughout my day to guide my steps, in Your name and for Your glory!*

*Thank You, Jesus, for Your promises and the blessings in my life.*

*In Jesus's name, I pray.*

*Amen.*

# Dear Lord,

*Lord, let me remember to call on You today. Give me the wisdom and the strength that only comes from You. Lord, help me to grow closer to You in faith, faith that is deep and never wavers, that doesn't look for answers of tomorrow but trusts in You so much that being in the here and now is enough.*

*Lord, open my heart to Your love and direction for me with unquestionable obedience.*

*Lord, let me have the peace through You that fills me with the inner tranquility that only You can provide. Fill me with the strength to stand firm in Your promises and against the enemy's feeble attempts to derail my faith in You. Make me new and wash me clean so that I can put on the armor of God.*

*I declare that I was born for now, to step out in Your Word and bring Your Word to others through my actions and thoughts.*

*In Jesus's name, I pray.*

*Amen.*

## Dear Lord,

*Forgive us all our sins today—sin that comes from being anxious, stressed, controlling, or lacking faith and hope.*

*Be with us. Open our hearts to Your Holy Spirit. Teach us to not get distracted by the enemy but to fix our eyes on You. Teach us to look up and remember that You are in control.*

*Lord, guard our hearts and protect each of us as we walk out tonight into the darkness. Fill each of Your warriors with the Holy Spirit to speak light to the one. Let us show the love and goodness that only comes from You. Let us be the light in their darkness, to be so bright that minds are turned to You, Lord, and away from the enemy's lies. Give us Your power to overcome those lies with Your truth, the truth that will set Your sons and daughters free. I declare that the truth that we speak tonight will set free those who are in chains.*

*All in Jesus's glory and in His powerful name!*

*Amen.*

# Dear Lord,

*Guide me today for Your glory, not mine.*

*Lord, teach me to be humble, the type of humility that comes from obeying and being solely dependent on You. Lord, teach me to be gentle, not to get angry, hurt, or frustrated by the actions and decisions of others. Keep me close to You and remind me every moment of every day. Lord, teach me to be patient, patience that outlasts the adversity that threatens to poke at my soul. Lord, You are my provider, my Jehovah Shalom, my Lord of peace. Show me the peace that I need to dwell in. Let there be peace in my heart that will shine hope for others.*

*In Jesus's name, I pray.*

*Amen.*

## Dear Lord,

*Please give me Your grace today to be patient and kind, to be present with love even when people around me are pursuing chaos. Help me to rise above the chaos and be righteous in Your name and only for Your glory. Teach me to make the right decisions today that lead to Your approval.*

*Lord, fill me with Your Holy Spirit so that only love comes from my mind, my heart, and my mouth.*

*Please steer me on the right path for all Your promises.*

*In Jesus's name, I pray.*

*Amen.*

# Dear Lord,

*I come to You this morning to give You all the praise and honor You deserve. Thank You, Lord, for all the goodness You have shown all of us.*

*Lord, let me feel Your presence today. I give You all my cares, worries, and burdens. I trust You, Lord, that You will take care of me.*

*Help me, Lord, to stay focused on You today with my heart and my mind, that everything I do today will be for Your glory. Help me speak love with grace to others so that I will receive Your peace, which is greater than anything I can understand. Today, I choose joy despite what may go on around me. Lord, strengthen me in Your power so that I may be a blessing to others who may be hurting. Almighty and merciful Lord, protect and guide me throughout the day. May all that I lay my hands on be successful in Your name. Help me see more of You and less of me.*

*In Jesus Christ's name, I pray.*

*Amen.*

And we know that in all things God works for the Good of those who love Him, who have been called according to His purpose. (Romans 8:28 NIV)

## Dear Lord,

When You are with me, there is no darkness. You don't have any shadows. Your love is pure. When we look around us, we can see so much brokenness and hear so much sadness. Bring Your light and presence. Let me shine Your light. Bring Your hope and be with me so that I can show Your hope to those who feel defeated. Let them see Your never-ending love and compassion through me. Please show me that it's more about You and less about me. Your light shines brightly on all we do if we turn away from any shadows of darkness. Nothing is lost when we have You in our lives. Please give me the patience to be still today and listen to Your direction for me, to slow down and breathe in and release all worries and concerns that try to threaten my day, to be renewed today in Your mercies. Lord, You are my rock. You are trustworthy, good, and the way for me to follow in my daily life. Give us Your light today.

In Jesus's name, I pray.

Amen.

## Dear Lord,

*Let me be patient with those You have brought to me. Please open their hearts so they can see Your love. Let me show them Your love, putting my judgments aside. I can get so consumed with what's around me and what's next when I need to let all my concerns go, slow down, and allow myself to be consumed by You. Teach me to rest in You, to find the answers that I need to see with my life every day, not to automatically try to solve everything. And, Lord, I need help to not get frustrated because it doesn't always go as I planned or how I think the outcome should be.*

*Lord, help me to be kind when I need to be truthful and direct. Lord, let those I love be truthful to me too.*

*Thank You for Your never-ending patience to me. With Your patience, I'm learning that every day I need to start again by putting on Your armor to face and live in this world. I need to believe, really believe, that I was born to make a difference in my lifetime through You, to those lost and hurting. Your want for me is to show hope through faith in You. Through this faith that I show others, my heart will come to know and feel You more.*

*Thank You, Jesus, for Your daily mercies over my life!*

*In Jesus's name, I pray.*

*Amen.*

## Dear Lord,

*Open my heart today and show me what is less than You. Show me what You want me to acknowledge and work on. Lord, Your love for me is perfect in every way. Why do I struggle with some people You put in my path? Why do I question their sincerity? I know I have no right to judge. Lord, let me show them I live like You intended. Love that is thoughtful, deliberate, and pure. Holy Spirit, please soften my heart and make it easier to show love to those who may not have pure intentions. Release me and show me how to let go and know they don't affect me. Lord, You go before me.*

*Lord, give me wisdom and patience today to listen when I shouldn't speak and to turn to You through the fog of things that the enemy tries to confuse me with. Lord, take my stubborn will and turn it to Your will for my good.*

*In Jesus's name, I pray.*

*Amen.*

And he will delight in the fear of the Lord. He will not judge what He sees with His eyes or decide what he hears with his ears, but with righteousness He will judge the needy with justice, He will give decisions for the poor of the earth. (Isaiah 11:3–4 NIV)

## Dear Lord,

*It's easy to quote Your Word or to read it every morning, but to live it requires careful and deliberate thought and direction from Your Holy Spirit. This is hard for me sometimes, in such an instantaneous, got-to-have-a-quick-answer world. Teach me to not have to be the first with an answer or a remark. Help me to be better at just being quiet and paying attention to those who can get left behind when I'm trying to get ahead. Lord, You have chosen us to be Your hands and feet, to be more like You, to not be boastful about ourselves but to be more Christlike and humble. Let me become a servant to others. Lord, open my heart to compassion for everything around me.*

*Jesus, in Your glorious name, I pray.*

*Amen.*

# Dear Lord,

*It's so easy to fall into the thinking that I was the one who chose You, that it was my decision to move toward You. How arrogant and prideful is that?! Lord, I know it was You who chose me. In my heart, as You teach me new things, I have learned that You tapped me on the shoulder and asked me to be on Your team. You give me such great peace when I let go and give You all my burdens. It's humbling and amazing, Lord, all at the same time. Lord, I know and I have experienced the power of Your Holy Spirit that resides in me. Lord, I know and believe that there is no darkness in me unless I let it in. There is no want for anything, unless I let that want in. Lord, let me shine Your brightness today. I rebuke any attempt by the enemy to confuse me while I walk the path You have me on.*

*Lord, I ask that You protect those close to me, the innocent, the faithful, the lonely, and the vulnerable, from any of the enemy's attempts to get to me. Lord, put Your solid hedge of protection around them and have Your angel armies surround them. We do not need to fear rejection, live in confusion, or wonder if we've missed out on a life meant for us.*

*Lord, I praise You with all my heart and thank You for all the goodness that comes our way today. It's all for Your glory, Lord. I am forever grateful!*

*In Jesus's name, I pray.*

*Amen!*

## Dear Lord,

*I ask that You renew our souls this morning, that the Holy Spirit will take control of our thoughts and actions. Lord, I put on Your armor to be righteous for Your laws, to know it is never my will but Yours. I trust in You! Lord, in Jesus's name, I rebuke all the attempts of fear and doubt that the enemy tries to play in my head.*

*The Holy Spirit guides me and helps me to rest in You. Let me give all the control to You in my thoughts and my actions. Teach me to be thoughtful and deliberate today, through Your powerful grace and love. Lord, only You can be my foundation, my rock. I am Your hands and feet today.*

*In Jesus's name, I pray.*

*Amen.*

# Dear Lord,

*Show me Your plan for today. Reveal to me all that is truly in my heart.*

*Lord, why is it so easy to rush to judgment?*

*Let the Holy Spirit guide me and let me rebuke that quick judgment and turn to You in thoughtful prayer instead of harsh judgment. I hand over all the negative thoughts and worries to You, Lord. I know I can work so hard, and at the end of the day, none of it really matters but how I am in Your eyes.*

*Lord, fill me with Your grace to understand where I'm at. Let me feel Your presence in this time of uncertainty and not predetermine the outcome. Let me just be. Show me how Your Holy Spirit, through me, can be a comforter to those who are suffering. Please also give me the love and patience I need for the oppressors and the foolish. I know You alone will be their judge. Give me the wisdom to speak to the foolish and to not let them harm or affect my path. Where their thoughtless behavior can be harmful or frustrating, I let go, and I'm resistant to judgment, criticism, and speculation that threatens to worm its way into my brain.*

*Lord, I give my life to You. Immerse me in Jesus's name!*

*I pray this in the power of Jesus Christ.*

*Amen.*

# Dear Lord,

*Wash me clean in the name of Jesus. Lord, reveal in me the gifts You have for others. I know that today will be less of me and more of You. I will mind my tongue. Lord, bless all those who I speak with today, with all Your glory and presence. Let it be Your light that shines from within me.*

*Lord, take away the struggles that I face. I constantly need to lay them at Your feet and not pick them up again. Lord, I know Your plan is working out for me. Deliver me today in Your grace and mercy to help me leave things alone and not control them. I praise You, Lord, and all Your glory. Lord, bless those who haven't yet found Your love, Your gifts, Your mercy, and Your Holy Spirit.*

*Lord, I rebuke the enemy and all his efforts to make me feel impatient, in Your name. Lord, take these thoughts away from me.*

*Lord, let me see all the beauty in everything and everyone. You are my constant, and I should never forget that for a moment. You are our sovereign Lord and can move mountains, as You always have. Things that happen in the natural are not what we should be sad or frustrated about. Turning to You, Lord, in these moments, we can see and feel the love and the promises You have for us.*

*In the power of Jesus's name, I pray.*

*Amen.*

# Dear Lord,

*Fill me with Your Holy Spirit. Give me the wisdom that only You can provide me so that I can obey Your commands and identify Your commands in my life. To have You so firmly in my heart and know the difference between Your plans and commands and those of my own stubborn will.*

*Lord, show me Your mercy when my will gets in my way, when my pride becomes so great that I can't even see Your direction for me.*

*Thank You, Lord, for all the blessings You have given me and continue to give me. Please bless and keep those in my heart safe from any harm today. Let them also see Your mercy in their lives.*

*Lord, guide us to do Your will in our lives today and not worry about yesterday or tomorrow, to place all worries and fears at Your feet and leave them there.*

*In Jesus's name, I pray.*

*Amen.*

## Dear Lord,

*Give me the humility that will bring me the peace that comes from trusting You. I know that in this time of confusion and while I walk through this valley, Your purpose for me is glorifying You before all the forces of this earth. This is for my own humility and growth in wisdom. Lord, forgive me when I want to give up on this pursuit and the path that You have me on when it gets tough. Looking at the seemingly impossible makes me realize that through You, anything is possible. Let me cling to You, Lord.*

*In Jesus's name.*

*Amen.*

## Dear Lord,

*Lord, I know I am here in my life because of Your love for me. You are the only one who decides where I go and what I do. You are the why in everything. Open my heart to Your will, not mine. I surrender all control to You. I rebuke my stubbornness. I rebuke all unnecessary worries. Free me from the anxiety of the unknown. Please break the chains that keep me from moving forward. You strengthen me through all You do in me. I praise You and give You all the glory for and in everything presented to me. Lord, fill me with Your Holy Spirit today and let me rest in You. Give me the discernment to know which path You are guiding me on. Give me Your grace to pause and breathe in Your direction for me, Your goodness for me. Help me not to get caught up in second-guessing and questions that aren't even to be answered. Lord, I have the faith in You to trust You. I give You all of me.*

*In Jesus Christ's name, I pray.*

*Amen.*

# Dear Lord,

Let Your Holy Spirit fill me today. Lord, I know You are merciful and forgiving. I know You will provide for me when I ask. I need Your strength and guidance to help me to overcome. You can move mountains that threaten to block my path and try to deter me in a different direction. You are all that I need in my life, my alpha and omega. I'm not the perfect one, and at times I sin, knowing that I am sinning. My actions and thoughts are never hidden from You. But even through all that, You still love me, and I know I am forgiven. Each morning, I can start again on Your right path. Give me Your strength and wisdom to get through this day. Lord, take my stubbornness and replace it with Your grace. Show me to rest at Your feet rather than compete when situations arise in my day. It's so exhausting and not fulfilling. Lord, it's in Your name I pray.

Amen.

## Dear Lord,

*Forgive me for having doubt in You, any amount of doubt that You are not who You say You are, or that You are capable of anything. We are so quick to lose faith in what we think or see as impossible, doubting that You can give us the strength and grace to do anything. We automatically let the enemy in and the doubt of whether we are good enough or smart enough to get whatever it is done. It's so easy to slip back into the old way of thinking. But if we would just hand over that doubt and make room for the kind of faith we need to have to believe in things unseen, our reward would be so great. Jesus, we get so caught up in wanting to see everything instead of just believing and knowing in our hearts that You are in control and that the faith and love we need to have in You and all that is yet to be is already in us. Lord, we are so grateful for all that You have done in us, and we ask for that continued growth of faith. Holy Spirit, guide us.*

*In Jesus's name, we pray.*

*Amen.*

## Dear Lord,

*Give me the courage and strength to see You as You are, to love You for Yourself alone, to expect Your miracles and to be patient for them. Let me have the eyes in my heart to also see Your glory by faith alone. Let my encounter with You smother any excuse, demand, or complaint that I may have in my heart.*

*Lord, You know what's in my heart, and it's in Your timing that You will show me the way. Lord, please reveal what's in my heart that is preventing me from seeing, and show me what I need to know and face.*

*"Be strong and courageous, do not be afraid or terrified because of them, for the Lord Your God goes with you; he will never leave you or forsake you" (DT 31:6), and in turn Lord, I will not forsake You. You are the foundation I stand on. My adamant!*

*In Jesus's name, I can do all things!*

*Amen.*

## Dear Lord,

*I surrender all to You and Your will. Please guard my heart today and shut my mouth to every negative thought. Forgive my transgressions and show me the mercy of Your promise. May the blood of Jesus cover our homes and Your servants today.*

*In Jesus's name, I pray.*

*Amen.*

## Dear Lord,

Let me release my prideful ways and trust in You. I know You have my back. I know You work all things for my best. But my own mental limitations always get in my way. Lord, I want and need You to reveal to me each time I get in my own way. Your glory is all I want to seek. I know You are in command and control of the future. Give me the grace and wisdom to rest in Your arms and drop everything at Your feet when life is so out of control in front of me. I believe that Your love conquers all things, and through You I can show that same love to others, even when my first thought is to judge and become prideful. Humble me. Give me the daily faith to focus only on You, no matter what comes my way. In Jesus's name, I pray.

Amen.

## Dear Lord,

*Reveal what's in my heart that is keeping me from my destiny today. Those things that I don't want to look at, let me see them and deliver them to You. Help me to love the vulnerable and not add to their vulnerability by walking past them. Lord, let Your Holy Spirit be in me today. Let Him guide me through all I do, giving up control and my will. Lord, You know what's in my heart, and only through You can it be washed clean. It's only from my heart that I should listen. Let my heart lead, not my mind. With the truth of the Holy Spirit, make my heart whole through You, my redeemer. Lord, don't let me put anything or anyone above You. Cut the areas of my heart that don't bear fruit and let only the healthy branches flourish and cling to Your vine.*

*Lord, I find peace in Your Holy Spirit, which is in me. I praise You for all Your glory and the mercies that You have given to me.*

*In Jesus's name, I pray.*

*Amen.*

## Dear Lord,

*Give me the wisdom to always surrender to You in times of crisis, no matter how small the crisis may seem. Fill me with Your Holy Spirit and the peace of mind that only the Holy Spirit can give. Be with me today. I hand over all my controlling ways to You. I need You in my life today. I know that until I make major adjustments, I will keep hitting that wall. Lord, show me all the adjustments I need to make, not just those I see with my eyes but those I have in my heart. It will be uncomfortable, but I want to be closer to You, and these are small sacrifices to obey. I will trust in You with my whole heart, to be all in, not just in the parts that aren't so scary but all of it. Give me the strength to not settle for the same old, same old, letting go of my old life to live the new life You have for me.*

*Lord, it's for Your glory.*

*Amen.*

## Dear Lord,

*You know my heart, and You know I love You. I'm trying to do my best to follow after You, but sometimes I get tripped up. Sometimes I lose focus. Sometimes I forget who I am in You, and I start looking to the world to tell me who I am, trying to be more like what the enemy wants. On those days when I have lost confidence, build me up again, Lord. Fill me with Your Holy Spirit and remind me of the simple truth that true confidence can only be found in You. I can walk around confident, knowing I am loved. I can walk around knowing I am enough. I can live each day knowing I have been rescued and am free and called to do great things I don't see right now. I know if I follow You, You will take care of me. Lord, help me and remind me of all those things!*

*In Jesus's name, I pray.*

*Amen.*

Trust in the Lord with all your heart and do not lean on your own understanding in all your ways submit to Him and He will make your paths straight. (Proverbs 3:5–6 NIV)

## Dear Lord,

*Give me an open heart to see what and who You see. Give me the patience to sit quietly, trusting and reflecting on You instead of reacting when the enemy tries to tell me lies and tear down my confidence. I know things will not go as I see them but always how You have planned them.*

*Lord, I praise You for the blessings You give me. I know You are always with me.*

*Lord, remind me to live through You in everything I do today. Remind me to put on my shield and keep it on at all times, rebuking the enemy who tries to prey on my weaknesses. I rebuke all the lies and put my life in Jesus's hands. I know that all I have to do is call Your name, Lord, and You protect me. Bring me Your peace and wisdom. In Jesus's name, I pray and declare this to be true!*

*Amen.*

## Dear Lord,

*Open our hearts and fill them with only Your love. Let the Holy Spirit guide us and Your angel armies surround and protect us.*

*Lord, don't let us get caught up in the lies and the noise, but let us make the major adjustments in our lives to be able to follow You, to be more like You and fulfill the promises You gave us. We are branches on Your vine, and we want to be fruitful, but at times we listen to the noise. Please prune back the areas where we aren't fruitful and deliberate for You. Give us Your unfailing strength to stand strong on the rock and Your love, Lord. Not our level of love but Your level, to show others You live in us, to be the hope and to always glorify You, Lord. Reveal those who are vulnerable today and need You. Don't let us walk past and not see them.*

*In Jesus Christ's name, I pray.*

*Amen.*

## Dear Lord,

*Be my strength today. Show me and lead me, Lord, where You want me to be. Lord, I stand firm on the rock in Your presence. Let me humble myself and teach me wisdom today to discern what You have placed before me and what You haven't. Wisdom to know when to share You with others, to know how and what to say to someone in need, to identify the vulnerable. Lord, with Your Holy Spirit, I have peace and comfort that anything is possible. Lord, I'm letting go of the control and clinging to hope and faith in You. I know that right now I am in the wilderness, but I'm not afraid because I know You are with me and haven't forsaken me. Lord, build my confidence through You so that whatever comes my way today will be faced as a blessing and I will give You all the glory every time and in every situation.*

*In Jesus's name, I pray.*

*Amen.*

## Dear Lord,

*Heal my heart, open my heart, and make it clean today. Open my eyes to the things unseen. I have faith in those things unseen and yet to be seen. I know Your Holy Spirit works in me for Your glory. I know that the frustrations or unknowns that I'm experiencing today are just a small blip in Your overall plan. No person can deny me of what is in Your plans for me.*

*Show me how to love others unconditionally as You love me, Lord. It's not always easy to do. Continue to show me Your grace. Everything I do today will be for Your glory and for the sacrifice You made for me. Lord, thank You for the time I spend with You. Fill me with Your Holy Spirit to speak Your words and declare Your goodness and love.*

*In Jesus's name, I pray.*

*Amen.*

Let us hold unswervingly to the hope we profess, for he who promised is faithful. (Hebrews 10:23 NIV)

## Dear Lord,

*Let us remember that no sin against us will ever be at the level of the sins that were brought against You this day, and that we should forgive those sins. Lord, today is a day of mixed emotions. Good Friday was the reality to share the Good News that Jesus died for us. I can get so caught up in why someone would treat an innocent man that way. But You hardened their hearts so the scriptures could be fulfilled, because it is always Your will and not ours. With His sacrifice, You showed us how much You truly love us. Lord, I lay down all my sins, my worries, my stress, my focus on what's unimportant, my concerns about tomorrow, my anxiety. Keep them and bury them with all the transgressions that You took away for us. Fill me instead with Your Holy Spirit so others will see that You have risen to spread within us the Good News. You give the same blessings to all who believe in You, the sacrifice You made to fulfill God's will and promise. There is nothing but praise to You that will come from my mouth today. Lord, bless us with Your presence today. Guide us and protect us. Fulfill Your will through us.*

*In Jesus's name and in His victory, I pray.*

*Amen.*

# Dear Lord,

*Fill me with Your Holy Spirit today. Guide me to do what's right in Your eyes, to fill my thoughts with You, and to make the purposeful decisions I need to make. Let me search my heart for what is true and correct first. Let the blood of Jesus Christ cleanse my conscience.*

*Lord, thank You for all the blessings You have given me and for all Your promises yet to come.*

*In Jesus's name.*

*Amen.*

# Dear Lord,

*Reveal to me what truly lies in my heart for others. Show me how to love everyone, even those who try to engage in anger or discourse.*

*Lord, I know that genuine love in my heart confirms my salvation through You. I know Your ways are higher than my ways. Give me the grace to lean back into You and rest, especially when the flesh wants to react to what's happening around me. My faith in You is my confidence that the hope I have every day and in everything will come to pass.*

*In Jesus's name, I pray.*

*Amen.*

# Dear Lord,

*Forgive me my transgressions.*

*Lord, I know that by Your grace, I am alive spiritually through You. I am loved by You. Even when my decisions are flesh motivated, You will forgive me with Your grace and mercy. They are endless.*

*Lord, I know that the same power that lies in Christ lies within me today. Open my heart and fill me with Your Holy Spirit, so I can continue to grow and become more alive in You, and You in me. I praise You through all the storms big and small. I know that when I'm in one, You are always there. You have me and go before me. You guide my every step. When things are unexplained, it's Your will that I need to trust in. Humble me with every step, that I can become who You want me to be, not what I think I should be. I trust in You Lord.*

*In Jesus's name, I pray.*

*Amen.*

## Dear Lord,

*I know You go before me and fight my battles. I know that with You by my side, I have nothing to fear. My hope in You will never fail. I will wait in You and draw my strength from You. Lord, fill me with Your Holy Spirit and give me the strength to continue and not get tired. Guard against the weaknesses and remind me of where my heart should always be.*

*Lord, I praise You for these moments and for the blessings yet to come. You never fail me.*

*In Jesus's name, I pray.*

*Amen.*

## Dear Lord,

I know the prince of this earth does not control or define me, and I rebuke his attempts and lies. You are my protector, my guide, my defender, and the only one who defines who I am and what my calling is. I know sometimes I don't show the humility or peace in my heart that I should. I let the current situation and my personal ambitions get in the way of what You want for me. Lord, I deliver all my pride to You, all my greedy thoughts of how I think it should be. As it is written, "Let me lead a life worthy of the calling I've received." Lord, I know You go before me and fight my battles. Give me the faith to let go, the trust to step forward, and the faith that You will always hold me in Your righteous right hand.

In Jesus Christ's name, I pray.

Amen.

## Dear Lord,

*Thank You for Your forgiveness of my transgressions and my sins from the past and those I will commit today.*

*Lord, Your power and mercy dwarf any anxiety or stress I may have. Bring me beside You and show me how loved I am.*

*Lord, I gain perseverance through You. Let me succumb to Your will and rebuke all temptations to do otherwise. Open my heart to accept others where they stand, and open their hearts to see what You do through me.*

*In Jesus's name, I pray.*

*Amen.*

## Dear Lord,

*I give You all the praise and glory for Your name! Lord, thank You for reminding me that Your Spirit truly lives in me—the Spirit that gives hope not just to me but to others, the light that shines in the darkness. It would be so much easier to sit here and listen to You all day, to sit in the quiet. But that's not what You have for me. I get so caught up in the unknown each day. I know my questions, my concerns, and my worries really amount to nothing. By being still and standing in Your light, Your love, I am reminded that everything else is just a distraction. I know that the will of my Father is stronger and my distractions really don't matter.*

*Lord, thank You for choosing me to walk this path, to be Your hands and feet today. Teach me to be in the present. I am strong only through You. No matter what comes my way, my strength will not change!*

*In Jesus's name, I pray.*

*Amen.*

# Dear Lord,

*I forgive myself of my sins, the sins of my heart that keep me from You. Each one is like a ball of sand that I throw in the ocean. I see each ball dissolve into specks and disappear. I know that You have me during this heat that surrounds me. You've told me it's going to be hot, but it won't consume me, and it will never define me. Lord, I stand firm in Your promises. My eyes will not leave Your face! I will always listen to You, and I trust Your words to me. You said to me, Selah.*

*I will pause and rest in You today. You will fight my battles. And when things don't make sense to me, I know I can turn to You. Praise You and all Your glory, and no harm will come to me. Lord, overfill me with Your Holy Spirit today.*

*In Jesus's name, I pray.*

*Amen.*

## Dear Lord,

We believe in Jesus's name, that You have taken all our sins and thrown them into the sea, blotted them out. They are no more. Give us the joy to live today sin-free. Lord, we pray for those who are suffering, discouraged, and oppressed by sin; for those whose dreams were shattered; for those who are sad and frustrated about things that are not in their control; for those who are lonely, wondering if anyone cares. We pray that You go near them and comfort them with Your Holy Spirit. We pray that You give us Your wisdom to be near them and to be faithful to Your Word while ministering to them, that their hearts will be open to Your Word. Lord, help us to be tuned into Your Word and allow us to speak through You. Let us listen to You, so we can be changed.

In Jesus Christ's name.

Amen.

> For this very reason, make every effort to add to your faith, goodness and to goodness, knowledge and to knowledge, self-control and to self-control, perseverance and to perseverance, Godliness; and to Godliness, mutual affection, and to mutual affection, love. For if you possess these qualities in increasing measure, they will keep you from being ineffective and unproductive in our knowledge of our Lord Jesus Christ. (2 Peter 1:5 NIV)

## Dear Lord,

*I ask that You show me how to have the level of love and joy that is in You.*

*Today, Lord, I want to show love to those who are hard to love, to be Your servant today and walk in the path that You have for me, to come to those who feel unloved and unworthy and be Your deliverer of love, the level of love that only You can give.*

*Today, Lord, show me the kind of joy that only comes from knowing You. Give me the grace to show others that joy. I will rejoice that through good and bad times, You are always with me. You have never forsaken me. Show me how to help the one who is lost. Through me, show them how to find You and their own path to You, to find the real joy that only comes from You.*

*In Jesus's name, I pray.*

*Amen.*

## Dear Lord,

I know that You love me where I am. Your amazing grace is always there for me no matter what I think or do. Lord, I know my doubts and fears are not real, but they always threaten. Give me the strength to overcome them. I know You chose me and I belong to You. You opened my eyes and my heart to Your Word and Your blessings. Let me be better at resting in all of You. Lord, I praise Your glorious grace! Thank You for giving me this day. Help me not to waste it but to walk in the light and to do Your will, to show that one how Your mercy is endless. Fill me with Your Holy Spirit to fulfill Your promises here on earth. Lord, You brought me out of the darkness that ruled my life and into the light that now shines down on me. Let me show others today the hope that is You.

In Jesus's name, I pray all this to be true.

Amen.

## Dear Lord,

*Give me strength. Help me not to lean on my own understanding but in everything to submit to You and acknowledge You so You can direct my thoughts and actions. Lord, please inflame my heart with Your love and enlighten my mind with the truth, whether it's what I want or not. Lord, my heart is filled with chaos and confusion. Please give me the strength and peace that only You can give. May Your will be done. No matter what, I know You are by my side. You, Lord, will have the final word. Cleanse us of our unrighteousness, wash us clean, and heal us from the inside out. Your grace is all I need.*

*In the name of Jesus Christ.*

*Amen.*

# Dear Lord,

*Reveal to me what my heart is holding on to. Help me throw all that is hidden and negative and discouraging in the ocean.*

*Lord, bless those who need Your healing. Give them rest in Your arms. Let every care, concern, and worry leave them. Fill them with Your Holy Spirit today. Comfort them and keep them close to You. I know that when You shine Your face on them, they will feel the warmth of Your love.*

*In Jesus Christ's name, I pray.*

*Amen.*

## Dear Lord,

*Fill me with Your love today. Let me show the hope I have in You to others.*

*I know You're guiding me for Your glory, although sometimes it feels as if things are just standing still. It feels like every day I'm on repeat. Lord, reveal in my heart what You want me to see and work on. Have mercy on me when I don't see it.*

*Lord, I have faith in You that You will always provide, no matter what.*

*In Jesus's name, I pray.*

*Amen.*

# Dear Lord,

*It's not easy when the enemy brings so much to mind. But I know and have seen Your forgiveness. You lifted me out of the darkness so long ago, and Your mercies and grace have been given to me without hesitation. Lord, let me be able to give mercy and grace to others without hesitation. I know You also want nothing but goodness and abundance to fill my day.*

*Lord, I praise You and thank You for the promises You have given me that are yet to come.*

*I put on the armor of Your truth and justice this morning, renewing my heart to face any challenges with You by my side. I can do all things through You.*

*I pray this in Jesus's name.*

*Amen.*

## Dear Lord,

*I commit myself to not be tossed around by my thoughts and emotions in the circumstances I am in, in any moment. I commit to You, whether I'm faced with a mountain or walking in a valley. You have not forsaken me. You are always with me. I will reach out my hands and cling to You.*

*Lord, let my faith grow through perseverance during this season. Let me release my hold on how I think things should be. Let me walk behind You. I commit to letting go of the control today. Your will be done.*

*In Jesus's name.*

*Amen.*

## Dear Lord,

*Thank You for giving me the strength and the grace to forgive others.*

*Lord, help me to consider the trials in my life as nothing but joy. Help me to use them as an opportunity to draw even closer to You. Help me to understand what You are trying to teach me through these trials, and help me to realize they are necessary if I want to become mature and complete in my faith.*

*Lord, use me for Your glory. I know that means trials are inevitable, so help me to walk through each one faithfully committed to You. Let me fulfill Your promises to expand Your kingdom.*

*In Jesus's perfect name, I pray.*

*Amen.*

> Refuse to worry about tomorrow, but deal with much challenge that comes your way, one day at a time. Tomorrow will take care of itself. (Matthew 6:34 TPT)

# Dear Lord,

*Thank You for being by my side through every trial. Thank You for creating purpose out of my pain. Thank You for the message out of my mess. I know that my response to any adversity and challenge is within my control today. Lord, I speak victory over myself today. I believe that I will make it through this and any spiritual workout. I believe that everything I am supposed to learn during this process will come to pass. Lord, I honor You. I put my faith, hope, and trust in You.*

*In Jesus's name, I pray.*

*Amen.*

## Dear Lord,

*Search my heart and reveal to me what walls I've put up that prevent me from moving forward. Lord, the trials are tough, but I trust in You. I give You my heart. I trust that You will use these trials, this spiritual warfare, for my good. It's Your greater purpose that will prevail, more than I can fathom. Let Your will be done. Remind me to stay out of my own way when fear tries to take over. Help me to stay obedient. Help me to stay faithful, from the beginning of my day until I close my eyes at night. Use my life for Your glory.*

*In Jesus's name, I pray.*

*Amen.*

# Dear Lord,

*Open their hearts with Your mercy. Blind them from the enemy.*

*Lord, I come to You in confidence. I receive Your grace and mercy. I receive all the blessings You have given me and will give me.*

*In exchange, I give You my heart.*

*In exchange, my flesh died on the cross, and I've been reborn new.*

*In exchange, I pick up my cross and follow You.*

*You have not forsaken me!*

*You will never leave me!*

*Your Holy Spirit fills me and directs my every step.*

*Your grace and love light my path.*

*In Jesus's name I declare this to be true.*

*Amen.*

## Dear Lord,

Thank You for the blessings You have given us, the strength that only You can provide us. Lord, let each of us be joyful through all the enemy tries to send us. We are stronger through You, stronger than the enemy's attempts could ever be. Our faith and hope in You, our confidence in You, out measures anything that tries to make us stumble and fall. Lord, You have our hearts.

In Jesus's precious name, we pray.

Amen.

## Dear Lord,

Protect those who are loved by You and those who love You with their whole heart.

Lord, may nothing separate me from You today. Teach me how to choose only Your way today so that each step leads me closer to You. Help me to walk by Your Word and not by my feelings. Help me to keep my heart pure and undivided. Protect me from my own careless thoughts, words, and actions. Keep me from being distracted by my wants and my desires, especially my thoughts on how I think it should be. Help me to embrace what comes my way as an opportunity rather than an inconvenience. Remind me not to put myself ahead of You. I put Your promise of absolute love in my heart.

Thank You for all Your blessings and the gift of having a relationship with You. Thank You for the power of You in my life forever.

In Jesus's name, I pray.

Amen.

# Dear Lord,

*It is true that as I believe, so will I live. But it is also true that as I live, so will I believe. If I act in love and faithfulness toward You, I sense love from and to You growing in my heart. So test me and provoke me, by Your Spirit, to ever obey and serve You, regardless of my state of mind or emotions. Lord, help me to get my eyes off the mountain before me and put my eyes on You, the God who moves mountains. Teach me to always look up into Your face, rather than down at the long path I'm on. Eliminate the panic and the anxiety that the enemy likes to so easily weave into my life each day. Give me the strength to walk on the water with You, to not just trust in what I can see but to rely on You only. Lord, You are worthy of my trust.*

*In Jesus's name, I pray.*

*Amen.*

## Dear Lord,

You have always been by my side, no matter what. You have been there to give me the grace I need. Lord, continue to tell me, show me, and teach me, by Your grace, all the fruits received by the Holy Spirit. By Your grace, I have all the skills I need to do all You ask me to do with ease.

Lord, I celebrate Your presence in my life today. Continue to help me build my foundation in You and on You. You are my adamant!

In Jesus's name, I declare this to be true!

Amen.

## Dear Lord,

Let me forgive those who have sinned against me. Lord, thank You that Your love for me is patient when I'm not perfect. Thank You that all You have and ever will speak to me is truth. May Your truth be spoken through me in only faith and love.

Lord, Your grace strengthens me, and Your armor protects me. With You beside, before, and behind me, I have no fear.

Lord, it's Your love and truth that fill me. Guide me in that truth and show me what You have for me to do, in Your name and for Your glory.

Your face shines on me, and Your Holy Spirit fills me.

In Jesus Christ's name, I pray.

Amen.

"No weapon formed against me will prosper."

# Dear Lord,

*Holy Spirit, fill me and guide me. Show me how to rejoice in any trial I face today, big or small. Teach me to not become proud of accomplishments but to always rely on Your truth and love through Your victories. Lord, guide me to persevere when the going gets tough and lonely. Let me always remember that You are with me every step of the way. I know that in my business life, there are always going to be people who don't believe in You and all Your glory. Lord, help me to forgive and bless them and not forsake them for not believing. I am thankful for those You have placed before me who do believe in Your glory. Help me to continue to be strong in You and to always stand firm against the enemy.*

*In Jesus's name, I pray.*

*Amen.*

# Dear Lord,

*Teach me to not judge others but to love them as You loved me, to forgive them for what they do, as Jesus forgave us. Guide me with Your grace.*

*Lord, fill me with Your mercy to be merciful to others so that they can see You in me. Reveal to me what grows in my heart and help me learn from it, to conquer what is wrong and to bloom what is good, to show love to others. Rest my thoughts and tongue so that nothing but grace and wisdom are heard.*

*In Jesus's name, I pray.*

*Amen.*

## Dear Lord,

Help me to put on my armor every morning, every time. Rebuke the enemy that tries to distract me with other things. Nothing is more important than the time with Your Word and the Holy Spirit.

Lord, let me soak in every word that I read this morning. Let me have a freshness of the Holy Spirit so I can bring Your love that is alive in my heart and flowing through my life. I know I can't do it on my own. I don't have the strength within me. Only through You is it possible. I need to show others what Your love, true love, looks like. Protect my heart from the daily frustrations that try to rob me of my peace and joy.

Lord, if I do good deeds or sacrifice every day, but I don't have love in my heart, it means nothing.

Lord, grant me Your love today.

In Jesus's name, I pray.

Amen.

# Dear Lord,

*Thank You for this day before me. Forgive me of my sins and forgive those who sin against me.*

*Lord, let me live righteously today in Your name. Let me be a blessing, not a curse, to those I see today, those I can see through Your eyes. Open my eyes to those in need. Open my heart and fill it with the Holy Spirit. Reveal to me what I'm lacking. Reveal to me what I should be giving, to be someone who truly follows You, not someone who just talks about it. Humble me and give me the grace to show others Your generosity.*

*In Jesus's name, I pray.*

*Amen.*

## Dear Lord,

*I praise You for all that You are. You create the sunrise every morning and the sunset every evening. Your glory and splendor, in the tiniest creation to the highest and largest mountain, is worthy of all the praise I give You. You are my Jehovah Shalom, the Jehovah Jireh, my Father. Thank You for all things You've done in my life, all for my good.*

*Lord, forgive me of my sins. Forgive my worries and anxieties, the heaviness that I allow to sit on my heart. All these things are out of my control. All these things are what the enemy wants to scare me with. I rebuke them all. Lord, You and only You are the one in control of my life. You always have me in Your hand. Lead me to the peace and contentment that only You can give.*

*In Jesus's name.*

*Amen.*

## Dear Lord,

*I praise Your glory. I praise all that You do for us and all that You bless us with every day. Lord, forgive my heart and mind for judging people I don't even know, and forgive those I meet who judge me. Open our hearts to see and hear You, to hear Your direction for us.*

*Lord, I ask You to be in my presence today, to give me wisdom and grace through all the decisions that come my way. Give me the right words to come out of my mouth—words that are healing, not hurtful. May every thought in my mind be pure and loving, not anxious and fearful.*

*Lord, I yield to You the day. What do You want me to do for Your glory?*

*In Jesus's name, I pray.*

*Amen.*

# Dear Lord,

*We bless You for our lives. We give You praise for Your abundant mercy and overflowing grace that we receive each day. We thank You for Your faithfulness.*

*Lord, forgive us for the times we struggle with our faithfulness, when we try do to things our way.*

*Lord, we know that all things are Yours. We know that You are always in control, not us. You are able to keep, take care of, and bring to pass the things we commit to You in prayer.*

*Lord, we come boldly as Your daughters and sons and ask for Your guidance and protection from all the forces that despise peace and righteousness, that each step we take toward truth will show others love and Your unlimited grace, mercy, and hope.*

*In Jesus's victorious name.*

*Amen.*

## Dear Lord,

*I declare that Your angel armies are surrounding each of us today. We are Your warriors to spread Your light in the darkness. Holy Spirit, open our hearts to be humble, to listen to those who are lost. Show them through us how warm and inviting You are, that You are hope in their darkness, the deliverer of all who come before You with humbleness. Lord, there is one who needs to be found tonight. Let us plant the seed and hand them to You to love and protect. I praise You, Lord.*

*In Jesus's beautiful name, who rescues the lost.*

*Amen.*

## Dear Lord,

*Thank You for all the blessings You have given me. Your will be done on earth as it is in heaven.*

*Forgive me, Lord, for my thoughts of transgressions. Give me the strength to rebuke those thoughts immediately and deliver them all to You. The enemy has no power.*

*Lord, through my crisis of belief, I know I make decisions that show You whether I trust only myself or depend absolutely on You. I know that I must act on the purposes that You reveal to me. When You show me the tasks that are God size, keep me from the temptations to choose the tasks that are me sized. Lord, I want the world to see You at work through me. I know that the only way this will happen is for me to give everything over to You and to trust in You wholly. Help me today to obey and to trust. I will follow You today, Lord, no matter what the result is.*

*In Jesus's name, I pray.*

*Amen.*

## Dear Lord,

*Thank You for all Your goodness and wisdom, even in our darkest valleys. Lord, thank You for all the grace and mercy that You show me. Thank You for these brief moments of peace.*

*Forgive me, Lord, of my sins, and let me forgive others as You have forgiven.*

*Lord, I ask that You are with me today to help me make wise decisions, to find joy in all that I do, to not be afraid of anything but deliver all fear and doubt to You.*

*Lord, please show mercy to those who need Your love and embrace. I open myself to all that You ask me to do today. Let me be Your hands and feet, showing grace and kindness in Your name.*

*In Jesus's name, I pray.*

*Amen.*

## Dear Lord,

*You are my breath, my light, my fortress every moment. Let me remember this always. In the face of adversity, let me know You have me in Your right hand.*

*It's so easy to get caught up in this world and to be so concerned about ourselves and what the world has to offer us, to make sure we get our fair share. Lord, stop us and have us look to the people outside our comfort zones. Have us reach out to them by being Your hands and feet, to walk on the path You already have for us.*

*Lord, open our hearts and minds today. We rebuke all that the enemy tries to put in our way. Help us turn our circumstances for Your goodness and mercy on others.*

*I declare freedom from all the negative situations.*

*Let us find peace and comfort in Your presence. You are all we need each day. You are our Jehovah Shalom!*

*In Jesus's holy name, I pray.*

*Amen.*

# Dear Lord,

Thank You for Your grace and Your generous blessings, Your creations on earth that we see every day. From each morning's sunrise to the people we come in contact with, Lord, let me see those people as Your creations. Keep the worries and negative thoughts of these people from me. They were all made in the likeness of You. Lord, forgive me for thoughts that do not promote love. Fill me with Your Holy Spirit so I can see them as You do.

Lord, please guide us, Your sons and daughters, to look outside our insignificant daily worries and see the vision You have for us, to not make it complicated but to act in Your name and for Your glory always.

Lord, I am open to Your Word, Your grace, and Your wisdom. Guide me today to Your will, not mine.

In Jesus's name, I pray.

Amen.

# Dear Lord,

*I praise You for all the blessings You have given me. You have chosen me to walk on Your path, not to pass judgment on anyone, not to feel superior to anyone, but to love unconditionally everyone, no matter where they are or in what circumstance. Lord, open their hearts.*

*Lord, Your Holy Spirit fills me with Your grace and wisdom. It's never me Lord, always You. I will put on the armor of God this morning to again go out in this world and see with only Your eyes and hear with only Your ears. Guide me today. Lord, it's only You that I worship; no other person or thing will I put before You. You are my constant, the one who has always gone before me, behind me, and beside me. You have never forsaken me. I am Yours.*

*In Jesus Christ's name, I pray.*

*Amen.*

## Dear Lord,

*Thank You for the blessings You have shown me, even when I wasn't entirely perfect. Lord, You always forgive me. Lord, I know You see what's in my mind, and I know You see what is in my heart. Open my mind and reveal to me what I am storing in my heart. You know what lies ahead. Take away the pride that always blinds me. Take away all my will and help me to see that even though it doesn't always feel good, it is all for Your glory and my good. Take the "why me" away, Lord, and show me how to focus on the blessings of every situation, not the problems I face. Guide me, Lord, as You always have done. I know in my heart that all things have led me to the here and now. You have me on this path for a reason that is greater than I can even imagine. Help me to understand that the only relationship that matters is mine with You.*

*I will be still and listen to You. Lord, give me the wisdom to be still in Your presence and not jump to conclusions or rabbit holes in my brain. Teach me to wait for Your solutions. Open me to Your Word and keep me open to Your Holy Spirit every moment of today. I will yield to him and obey Your guidance.*

*To my Yahweh Shalom, my Lord of peace, I pray.*

*Amen.*

# Dear Lord,

You are the great I Am. You are the one who gives hope to the hopeless. Your infinite love shows in all You do.

Lord, let Your love shine on those who are lost today. Let them see Your greatness in their lives. Show them that we can all see Your glory if we have faith and hope, if we believe with all our hearts in Your glory and sacrifice for our good. Guide us to rebuke any temptations that the enemy tries to put in front of us and instead fulfill the assignments You have for each of us today.

Let us be victors and not victims!

In Jesus's name, I pray.

Amen.

## Dear Lord,

*I know You're here. I know You're always with me. And because I know Your heart, I can trust that the negative things I'm hearing aren't ever from You. I render them powerless in my life and ask You to remind me of the truth, that You are the I Am in me and who I am through You. Thank You, Lord, that You defeated the enemy already and he has no power. Show me where I need to stand firm; teach me that You fight my battles for me.*

*Thank You, Jesus, for never leaving me to fight this battle alone. You are always with me. I just need to look up and not lose focus on You.*

*In Jesus's name, I pray.*

*Amen.*

## Dear Lord,

*I praise You for all Your grace and mercy! For Your goodness and glorious gifts! For the peace I find in only You. You are my Jehovah Shalom! Always.*

*Lord, I declare that Your angel armies are released today to surround each of my warrior sisters in Your name. With the belt of truth on, we are reminded who we are in You, and with the breastplate of righteousness, You will protect our hearts as we make God-given decisions, in Your name only. Lord, with our shoes of peace strapped on, we will receive restful tranquility everywhere we go. With our shields of faith, help us trust in You, Lord, no matter the circumstances today. We will put on firmly the helmet of salvation to protect our thoughts, keeping them pure and sound. We will not be distracted by Satan's attempts to derail our thoughts. Let us know Your Word so that our swords of spirit will lead us to speak Your truth over these girls tonight, to be thoughtful and kind to the men who work there, and to silently forgive the patrons who are lost there tonight in every situation. We will put each and every piece of armor in place securely to protect us from harm.*

*Lord, with locked arms, we step out in unity, to be Your hands and feet, to be a light in their darkness. Let Your glorious power be awakened so that with each step, we are more motivated and encouraged. We are robbing hell and setting captives free with each and every conversation, hug, and smile tonight!*

*In Your precious name, Jesus, I pray all this to be true, as given to me by the Holy Spirit.*

*Amen.*

# Dear Lord,

*Thank You for all You have blessed me with. Lord, I praise Your goodness and wisdom in my life. Let me praise You every moment of today.*

*Lord, please forgive me of my sins. Reveal what's truly in my heart. The things I can't see. The snares that get in my way. Let me only have You in my heart. It's so easy, and it happens so quickly when other things and what others think become more important than what You want for me. I am not You. Let me release the control and all the things that are not important.*

*Lord, I ask You to keep my heart pure and always focused on You. I will be on my toes. Let me push away all the bad thoughts that try to defeat me. Things always try to take over and put themselves above You. My heart is set on only You. Don't let my mind stray from what You want me to do. I know that with the power of the Holy Spirit, I can do anything and overcome any situation.*

*Lord, show me Your favor today, as it is in Your will, not mine.*

*In Jesus's name, I pray.*

*Amen.*

# Dear Lord,

*Thank You, Jesus! Thank You for all the gifts and blessings You have shown me.*

*Lord, I praise You for all that I see, all that You have made. Lord, please forgive my thoughts of worry and my actions that try to take over any situation. Forgive me for thinking that I'm in control. I let go of everything. Lord, give me Your grace to forgive and bless those who sin against me or You. Show me that letting go is Your way and Your will. Lord, I ask for Your favor today in all that I do. I ask for Your healing and comforting hands for those whose hearts are broken. Open their hearts to You. Don't let the enemy win by creating ill thoughts and anxiety. Protect and comfort them. Give them the Shalom that only You have.*

*Lord, I open my heart to You and the Holy Spirit. Reveal what lies in my heart. Reveal all the idols that I possess. Let them be dropped and replaced with only You.*

*In Jesus Christ's name, I pray.*

*Amen.*

## Dear Lord,

*Bless those who attempt to come against me and break my peace. Forgive me for not letting that go and forgive them for all that they say and do. Nothing can come between You and me. I won't let them take my peace.*

*Lord, when I find myself in the middle of a vicious, cruel storm, I need to remind myself that You, Lord, are at peace. You aren't surprised by the storm that threatens to drown me. You are in full control of the storms. Lord, if You are at rest, then I should be too. All I need to do is call on You, even in the middle of the seemingly dark conditions. Light will silence the dark. I must believe that the struggles I am facing, the frustrating adversity that comes at me, is simply refining me for my good. Thank You, Lord, for the peace I can have when I fully turn to You. I say yes, Lord, I will carry out Your will as You reveal it to me. Thank You, Jesus!*

*In Jesus's powerful name, I pray.*

*Amen.*

# Dear Lord,

*Thank You for all Your mercies and grace, for giving me protection against things unseen. Thank You for leading me to accept the authority of Your Word.*

*Forgive me, Lord, of my stubbornness and quickness to try to take over. Forgive and bless those in my life who cause me anxiety and stress. Keep me focused on You and not them. Remind me of the Gospel daily. Remind me that it's good for my soul and strengthens my heart. It can be so easy to complain, feel sorry for myself, or be filled with anxiety. But when I look toward Calvary and see the blood of Jesus pouring out for me, it becomes harder to be so self-centered. Gratefulness naturally builds up in my heart when I can do this throughout my day. I know I need to force my soul to look up. I bless You, Lord, with all my soul!*

*In the name of Jehovah Jireh, I pray.*

*Amen.*

## Dear Lord,

*We praise You! We are thankful for all You do for us. Your grace is never-ending. Lord, You are our foundation through any storm. It's our daily choice, our daily fight, our daily trial to whether or not we remember, realize, and live in Your reality.*

*Lord, You have given us every external blessing imaginable, to the point that we are full of bliss. In any storm, show us how to be sustained, empowered, and propelled into Your purposes, to not just see Your shelter as a hiding place from the storms. Lord, let us be more like You in the storm and walk on the water, keeping our eyes on You. Let us know how to inherit the spiritual riches that we didn't know were available before when we ask with all our heart and soul. Change us into a person of valor and destiny. Let any storm today become our finest hour as You complete Your work in us.*

*Your will be done.*

*In Jesus's name, I pray and commit my love to You.*

*Amen.*

## Dear Lord,

*Please give me Your righteousness today. Help me to be the example of Your Word and grace. As a follower in Your name, be with me today to show others the grace and forgiveness that You have given us. Lord, let me rebuke all the enemy's temptations for disruptive thoughts today. Let each of us put on our full set of armor to protect our hearts, souls, and minds to only love You.*

*Lord, I humble myself in Your presence. Teach us all to be intuitive to others, not to be only inward thinking but to reach out to those in need and to those in our community.*

*We declare all things Yours.*

*In Jesus's name, I pray.*

*Amen.*

# Dear Lord,

Holy Spirit, guide me through the day. Show me where You need me to be. Reveal to me what keeps me from Your table. Let me receive what I can't understand. Let me receive what I sometimes feel I don't deserve. I give You my whole heart without hesitation.

Lord, help me to know, feel, and see that by Your name all my sins have been washed away. Let me leave all doubt at Your feet every moment of every day. Teach me to be Your child of royalty and be at the table today.

In Jesus's name, I pray.

Amen.

# Dear Lord,

*I declare:*

*The Lord is the everlasting God. The creator of all the Earth. He never grows weak or weary. No one can measure the depths of His understanding. He gives power to the weak, and strength to the powerless. Even youth will become weak and tired.*

*And young men will fall in exhaustion.*

*But those who trust in the Lord will find new strength. They'll soar high on wings like eagles*

*They'll run and not grow weary*

*They'll walk and not faint. (Isaiah 40:28 NIV)*

*In Jesus's name, I pray all this to be true.*

*Amen.*

# Dear Lord,

*Thank You, Jesus, for all the gifts You have given me. Thank You for always being here with me, always by my side. Forgive me for forgetting that and letting the enemy whisper in my ear. They are all false lies. You are always the voice of reassurance deep within me, a voice that is always part of me. Remind me today when the wind blows that it's Your love that surrounds me and breathes life into my soul.*

*Lord, You are the voice to the voiceless, the calm and the storm. You will lift me up when I'm tired and give me strength to continue forward.*

*Lord, hold my hand and walk with me through the flames. You are good through all of it. Your love gives me the power to stand firm, whether it's against the enemies of this world or the challenges You want me to face. I will stand firm. I trust in You. You will protect me and never leave me. I love You with all my heart, mind, and soul.*

*In Jesus's name, I pray.*

*Amen.*

## Dear Lord,

*Pour the Holy Spirit into me, into my mind. Help me to imagine what my eyes can't see. Open my heart and my mind. I am open to seeing and hearing and experiencing things I've never experienced before. More love, more joy, more peace!*

*Holy Spirit, be our eyes right now. Today. Tonight. Be our ears, our sense of smell, of taste, of touch. We want more of You today. Turn around and rebuke any false beliefs or misconceptions about who You are and what You are able to do. Break our hearts open wide. Open our eyes and our minds to what You want us to see, to feel and experience with the eyes of our hearts, where so much more can be seen than just through our physical eyes.*

*Lord, bring us deeper into Your wonder and majesty today. Let us not only experience Your immense love but to be Your hands and feet tonight and show Your love to the lost but not forsaken.*

*In Jesus's name, I declare this to be true!*

*Amen.*

## Dear Lord,

*Thank You for all Your glory. I love You, Jesus. I trust You. You are more than capable of dealing with my circumstances today. You are kind. You are wise, and You are so good to me. You love me and know me better than I know myself. I know You always want the best for me. Forgive me when I don't let go. I trust You and Your ways. Help me to see You and see Your way. Keep my heart and mind open to You.*

*In Jesus's name.*

*Amen.*

## Dear Lord,

*I praise You. All the glory is Yours. You always make my path smooth when I turn to You. You restore my peace. Lord, remind me to always turn my heart toward You and not toward selfish gain or the pride that threatens to blind me. I am humbled to You. Lord, I stand firm and tall in Your presence. I know that I am Your daughter. It won't and never should be my will but Yours, Lord. I drop all my worthless worries at Your feet. I will not pick them back up. I watch them dissolve like the sand thrown into Your ocean. Lord, take any disgrace I fear and replace it with the victory that is Yours! "Your righteousness preserves me."*

*In Jesus's name, I pray and declare this to be true.*

*Amen!*

# Dear Lord,

*I praise Your goodness over me; no matter my circumstance, You are good.*

*Lord, I will let You fight my battles for me. I will only fight for You, Lord, not against the earthly battles. I place all my battles, all my worries at Your feet. Lord, I believe I am redeemed, that my life has meaning and that all things in my life will be used for my good. Lord, I have hope in everything I cannot see and that is yet to be seen. I trust in You, Lord, to show me Your righteous path. Despite any material failures that I see, I know You see only successes for me.*

*Open my eyes and my heart today to see only Your glory. Whether it's the wind on my face from Your angels' wings or a conversation with a proclaimed adversary, You will open or close my mouth to only speak from the Holy Spirit. You are my Jehovah Jireh! My provider!*

*In the name of Jesus, I pray.*

*Amen.*

# Dear Lord,

*I praise Your name! It is my resting place during the day.*

*Holy Spirit, be with me today. I lay down all my material things and all my heavy doubts and fears that keep me from seeing. Lord, I receive Your wisdom today, the wisdom and grace to be still and know You are in control. The wisdom that is pure, fruitful, and full of mercy. The grace to be forgiving in the face of adversity, to let go of the battles my ego wants to win.*

*Lord, I give You all the glory on the mountains and in the valleys.*

*In Jesus's name, it is true.*

*Amen.*

# Dear Lord,

Thank You for always being with me. Thank You for the blessings You have given me and will give me. I praise You, Lord, for the beauty You share with me every day.

Lord, I know it's You who gives me the power to stop grieving over my weaknesses. I want to be open to receive God's grace, strength, and power instead. I know that Your strength and power are made perfect in my weaknesses. I will not be so disturbed at my weaknesses and self-perceived shortcomings that I fail to recognize them as great opportunities for You, Lord. I will not give the weaknesses any power.

Lord, You are my rock. You always go before me and behind me. I need to let You be within me too. I will let You fight my battles.

I open my heart today to let You in, not just during the easy times but also during the tough times. I will not continue to drive the circumstances under my will. I yield to Your will.

In Jesus's name, I pray.

Amen.

## Dear Lord,

*I praise You. I praise Your goodness and Your patience with me.*

*Lord, You have called me for Your purpose, not my glory but Yours—a good, solid purpose that will be a wonderful example of who You are. As You have written, if I don't stand firm in faith, I won't stand at all. Forgive me for my doubts, for my crisis of belief in myself and the plans You have for me. Some days, it gets so confusing. I know that Your plans for me can only be accomplished when I give them my very best time, effort, and focus, using the gifts You have given me. Lord, I will not lose focus today, and I will keep my eyes on You. I will not look at tomorrow or yesterday with fear or regret. I know nothing I think will change them or make anything move faster. Lord, give me the strength to turn away from anything that seems easier. As a believer, I have a responsibility to develop the talent and gifts You have given me, no matter what and no matter where. I will not rebuke or forsake them. Let me be an example of You today.*

*In Jesus's name, I pray.*

*Amen.*

# Dear Lord,

*Thank You for Your blessings and for the love You give me. Thank You for Your direction and mercy. Lord, forgive me of my sins and shortcomings. Help me to be more like You, to forgive those who have sinned against me. I will not put my trust in others, only You. I will not care what others think about me, only what You think about me.*

*Lord, continue to reveal yourself to me in every area of my life. I welcome You into the depths of my journey and ask that You guide my every step. I know You created me for such a time as this. Don't let me waste Your purpose for me. Please use my gifts and talents to glorify You. Help me bloom right where I am and fight the distractions that try to move me out of the right here, right now. Lord, as I move forward, help me to discern which paths I should take with Your strength and wisdom. I want to always walk beside You.*

*Lord, thank You for Your promises.*

*In Jesus's name, I pray this.*

*Amen.*

## Dear Lord,

*I praise You for all Your goodness toward me. Lord, thank You for waking me up today, for anticipating and anxiously waiting for what You have for me today.*

*Lord, help me on my path to forgive others. Open my heart to hear and feel what You want me to see and understand.*

*Lord, help me be confident in everything that comes my way, to know that You are with me, to automatically default to that knowledge and confidence rather than react. Give me the confidence that is only found in You. I know that You live inside me. You fill my heart with unwavering faith, trust, and hope. I am a woman on a mission to serve You, to know You. I totally surrender and fully depend on You to guide me as I work really hard but with grace and resting in Your presence. Lord, make me the God-fearing woman You created me to be. Lead me to continue to live out my unique story that You planned for me, with trust and faithfulness. I will follow You with courage and boldness.*

*In the name of Jesus, I pray.*

*Amen.*

# Dear Lord,

*I praise You, Lord. Praise God that in Christ I can do all things, for He gives me strength. I praise Your goodness and mercy toward me. Lord, You are patient and kind, even when I reveal my shortcomings and struggles. Lord, show me Your strength so I can be genuinely merciful to those who anger me. Let me forgive them as You have forgiven me, not to judge or condemn to satisfy my wants but to bless them and love them. Your amazing grace is what I need to focus on. Please align my heart with Yours so that my heart can be compassionate toward others, not hardened. Fill me with Your courage and perspective so that my forgiveness is meaningful and true, so that those I encounter see a glimpse of Your mercy and grace.*

*In Jesus's name, I pray.*

*Amen.*

## Dear Lord,

*Thank You for being by my side through every trial, with every step. Thank You for creating purpose out of pain. Reveal in me all things that block me from getting closer to You.*

*Thank You for creating a message out of my mess. Lord, I speak victory over myself today. I speak victory over those who I meet today who need Your love and mercy. I believe I will make it and be stronger through the spiritual workout and trials You have for me. I believe that everything I am supposed to learn on this journey will help me grow and will teach me grace and wisdom. But most of all, it will teach me to love and forgive.*

*Lord, I honor You. I put my faith hope and trust in You, Jesus.*

*In Jesus's precious name, I pray.*

*Amen.*

# Dear Lord,

*We praise You! Lord, we are so grateful for knowing You! You are so good. You are the great I Am! Nothing that has happened or will happen is without You.*

*Lord, forgive us of our sins. Help reveal what lies in our hearts and let us hand it to You. Help us forgive and forgive again—as it is written, to forgive seven times seventy-seven.*

*Lord, we put on our armor today to defend against the spiritual forces. Be with us and guide us to those who need You, those who seek You and Your grace. Lord, bless all those who feel lost and forgotten. Through You, we can be a light for them. Lord, we boldly stand firm. I declare Your angel armies to be found before us and behind us. I declare that each of us will be filled with Your Holy Spirit to say only Your words to the one. With You by us, nothing can penetrate what You have put together. Loose the chains that bind the brokenhearted, the ones who feel defeated, the ones who are lost. Let us be Your hands and feet today. Guide us to them. We are Your warriors.*

*Lord, it's in Jesus's name, the name above all names, that I pray!*

*Amen.*

# Dear Lord,

*I praise You! I praise Your grace and Your wisdom. Thank You, Jesus! No one is greater than You!*

*Forgive me Lord, for any doubting and for any disbelief when I feel defeated. Reveal those challenges in my heart and make them known to me. Let me continue to walk this out, forward with forgiveness and mercy. After all, who am I to judge others?*

*Lord, be in my heart today. Thank You for the relationships You have given me, for the eyes You open, for the lives You ask me to touch every day, the seeds to be planted in Your name. Holy Spirit, continually fill me with Your love and Your patience. Show me every day to love as You love, as You command me to love.*

*In Jesus's name, I pray.*

*Amen.*

## Dear Lord,

Thank You, Jesus, for all the blessings You have given me. Thank You for the beautiful sunrises and sunsets. You paint the skies each morning so differently than the last. And the sun that sets is so brilliant, showing me Your promises of tomorrow in the golden sky.

Lord, let me have the strength and perspective to place my hope in heaven and offer mercy, compassion, and forgiveness to the wrongful, destitute, and proud. Let me carry Your grace so that heaven can meet earth through my life and draw others closer to You. Teach me to give grace where none is deserved. May I obtain access to the heart of my heavenly Father and forgive as He has forgiven, just as I seek and pray to love as He loves. May I be filled with the compassion of the Holy Spirit and Your overwhelming grace that You've always shown me. May I be filled with the courage and strength to reach past a wrongful action and forgive the person deep within my heart.

Lord, I yield to Your will. I remove myself from the seat of judgment.

I pray this in Jesus's glory!

Amen.

## Dear Lord,

I praise You and glorify You. You are my savior, my hope unseen. You have given me so much, and I am thankful. Lord, forgive me of my sins and forgive those who have and will sin against me, no matter the harm they bring or the sadness they try to send to me. My armor is on, and my shield is up.

Lord, You are the rain and the snow that quenches everything that was born into You. Let me walk in and practice Your Word daily. Let me intentionally hear what You want me to hear and to see through Your eyes what is lost. Lift up those who need to be cradled in Your arms and protected against all evil intentions of this world.

Lord, open my heart so that my soul is exposed to You, so that the Holy Spirit can stand on any void and fill it. Teach me Your ways, the ones You want me to know. My life is Yours. Show me where I'm to walk today.

In Jesus's name, I pray.

Amen.

## Dear Lord,

Thank You for all Your love for me. Thank You for giving me the hope and the faith that lives in me today, to know I am loved beyond compare.

Lord, forgive me my sins, my occasional doubts and less than confident thoughts. Let me forgive those who are not with You yet. Please let me show them Your love is endless and without any requirements. I can't control any of that, and I know I should stop trying to replace You with me, even if it's in my head.

Lord, bless and keep those I love on this earth.

Lord, I ask that whatever You have for me, whatever is to come, fill me with Your Holy Spirit who guides me, so that I can face anything with confidence and joy. No matter what this earth puts in my way, I always have You to be my mover and remover.

Lord, I am so blessed and grateful for all You've asked me to do. I will persevere with grace, with my faith in You and the confidence I need.

In Jesus's name, I pray.

Amen.

# Dear Lord,

*We praise You! We thank You for all the truths and blessings You have given us, for the wonderful day today that gives us hope. Lord, it's all In Your hands with Your mercy and grace. Lord, forgive us of our sins and forgive those who sin against us. Lord, give me the patience to deal with the things I have no control over, not with frustration and scheming but with gentleness and faithfulness. Build me up to face my challenges and hand them all over to You. Lord, open my heart to Your Word today. Fill me with the Holy Spirit so that I am not anxious about anything.*

*In Jesus's name, I pray.*

*Amen.*

## Dear Lord,

*I praise You for all the grace and mercies You give me, for Your power and wisdom, which control every situation. Lord, forgive me for forgetting that at times. Forgive me for being weak when faced with the enemy. Bless those who the enemy uses to frustrate and annoy me. When he tries this, please give me the strength to call it out and call on You. Remind me who You are in those moments and that You fight my battles. Remind me that Your plan for me is greater than anything said or done to me. It's not about me. Your words are greater than any words that come out of their mouth, or any lack of words from their mouths. Let me approach You with the faith and confidence that only the Holy Spirit can give me.*

*Still my soul so I can hear You, and still my heart so I can see You.*

*I drop all the things that are out of my control at Your feet. Help me not to be anxious in the quiet but to be still and peaceful, at rest in Your presence.*

*Lord, please give me the faith and encouragement today that comes when I am in You and You are in me.*

*In Jesus's name, I celebrate You!*

*Amen.*

## Dear Lord,

*I give thanks to You! To all Your glory, and I praise You! You are my rock and my foundation. Praise be to God for all Your grace and mercies!*

*Lord, forgive me for ever doubting the strength You have in my life. Forgive me for doubting what I cannot see or touch. Let my crisis of belief take me to the rock and be convicted in Your presence. I know that You don't ask us to compare our lives with others or to run someone else's race. Let me see myself as You have made me and feel the love that You have for me. Lord, let me cling to You and not to what is yet to be. Your perfect love casts out all fear and anxiety. Let me be secure in knowing that in every sorrow, every storm, and every joy, in good times and bad, You will never leave me. With You, I have the firm foundation to continue to build. Lord, I open my heart, my mind, and my soul to You today. Fill me with Your Holy Spirit, to be what You ask me to be, to obey without question or delay.*

*In Jesus's name, I pray.*

*Amen.*

# Dear Lord,

*Thank You for this day. I praise You and Your presence that surrounds me. Lord, forgive the ones around me who the enemy uses. I deliver all of them to You and rebuke his attempt to make me feel unstable and insecure. Your mercy is strong, and Your grace never-ending. Open their hearts to hear Your glory.*

*Lord, grant me the faith that moves me so that I can step out with trust that only You have, to fill the gap and do what only You command. The outcome is all Yours. I know that I get stuck focusing on only the things that I see, so open my eyes to see You at work around me.*

*Lord, open the eyes of my heart too so that I can see what You see and be where You want me. Guide my thoughts and my decisions. Holy Spirit, fill me and be with me as I walk this day out and declare it in Your name!*

*In the powerful name of Jesus Christ, I pray.*

*Amen.*

## Dear Lord,

*Thank You for Your love in my life. Thank You for all the blessings and for starting new every morning—a clean slate, a blank sheet of paper. I praise You in the stillness and in the chaos.*

*Forgive me when I doubt it, when I have a crisis of belief and forget that You can handle anything. Nothing is too small or too big for You. No one is outside Your love.*

*Lord, I declare my never-ending love for You. Lord, I am so grateful for all You have done in my life.*

*With an open heart and open soul, I commit to You today. Put on my armor to protect me from the unseen. I am Your child and cannot be shaken from that. I stand firm on the rock. Lord, be with me today, guiding my every step. Make my path straight and make all my actions for Your glory only.*

*In Jesus's name, I pray.*

*Amen.*

## Dear Lord,

*Glory to God! I praise You and all that You have done, are doing, and will do. Lord, keep my eyes focused on this moment, this day, not on anything past or anything future.*

*Forgive me of my transgressions. I rebuke all spirits of fear that try to seep in. Lord, You are my rock that I stand firm on. The Holy Spirit is the breath in my lungs. Your grace covers me.*

*Lord, give me the wisdom and grace to have Your words to speak when they're needed. Show me the difference. Lord, help me to not judge others but to give them that space they need to understand, and let me pray instead that they find You. Lord, I trust in You to help them. My hope comes from knowing You. The peace that fills me today is all because of You in my life.*

*In the name of Abba, our Father.*

*Amen.*

# Dear Lord,

*I am so grateful for all Your blessings. Your power overwhelms me. Anoint me and guide me today. Let me accept Your wisdom and mercy. Open my eyes to trust You with the decisions in front of me. Give me clear guidance in my life. Lift any fog that tries to surround me and any scales that cover my eyes. I submit myself to You. I know You will direct my path, and I have the confidence that Your direction is always best for me. You have never left me to wander through life, but instead, You have been so generous to me. Every moment of every day, You satisfy my every need. As Your child, give me wisdom today to glorify Your name in all I do!*

*In the name of El Shaddai, our Father.*

*Amen.*

## Dear Lord,

Thank You for Your wonderful blessings in my life! Your generosity to me has been beyond my imagination.

Lord, forgive me when my mind fills with doubt or concern about things I have no control over. My pride gets in the way of Your will. I release all my stubborn, flesh-gratifying thoughts to You. Reveal all contradictory thoughts, beliefs, or words of doubt that are not useful today. Thank You, Lord, for the spiritual gifts You have given me. I know You have given them to me for Your purpose and plan. Don't let me forsake them or belittle them, but help me grow them for Your glory. Lead me to use the fruits of the spirit every day and walk only in Your light, not mine. Let Your light shine through me to brighten others, lifting them up to You. Show me, Lord, what You want me to do, and I will obey.

In Jesus Christ's name, my King of kings!

Amen.

# Dear Jesus, our Lord and Savior,

*Thank You for all Your mercies and grace: for the sun that will rise today; for all the blessings You will give us today; for the joy, peace, and patience that I have the opportunity to claim and own. Lord, forgive me when I doubt, when I give in to the little lies and dark whispers that threaten to destroy my peace or my joy. Give me the strength to rebuke all those lies.*

*Lord, I am so grateful for Your grace that forgives me when I ask. Thank You for finding me and filling me with Your Holy Spirit.*

*Lord, heal any gaps with the patience to accept any delay, trouble, or suffering without getting upset or angry. Let me enjoy Your perfect peace in the middle of any chaos today. Send me the Word You have for someone lost. Let me know and feel how big You really are. Open the eyes to my heart so I can see how awesome You are.*

*In Jesus's powerful name.*

*Amen.*

# Dear Lord,

*Thank You, Jesus, for being the great I Am, for being all our glory and grace, for giving us new mercies every morning—new possibilities and new breath in our souls.*

*Lord, forgive me for my pride, for being boastful when I am nothing without You. Lord, help me to wash my heart clean and to soften my heart, to just be in Your presence. Help me to be humble and accept the things I can't change, to be patient for the things I can't see, and to understand that through You I am forgiven. Any shame or accusations have no place with me—no place in my heart, mind, or soul. I conscientiously throw them out and replace them with Your love and acceptance, with the joy and peace that only come from You. Lord, fill me with Your great commands to love You and to love my neighbor as myself, not to love and serve created things. Lord, to You all the glory.*

*In Jesus's powerful name, I pray.*

*Amen.*

> May the God of hope fill you with all joy and peace as you trust in Him so that you may overflow with hope by the power of the Holy Spirit. (Romans 15:13 NIV)

## Dear Lord,

*I praise You today for all Your glory, Your goodness, and the hope You give me. Lord, forgive me for my self-doubt. Forgive me for times I am ungrateful for the things You have done for me. Let me have such overwhelming faith and complete trust in You and what You have planned for me that others can see You through me. Let me press into the truth that through You I have received the greatest gift of all. It doesn't matter what I've done or how I think of myself, because You have forgiven me. I no longer have to carry the weight of sin or my failures. I can walk confidently in freedom, knowing that You broke the chains of rules and death. In You, I have everlasting hope and the promise of eternal life. Let me celebrate the peace You have given me, the Shalom in both my heart and soul.*

*Lord, today I ask You to fill me with Your Holy Spirit, to guide me in Your mission and purpose in my life.*

*It's in Jesus's name, I pray.*

*Amen.*

## Dear Lord,

Thank You for Your blessings on my life, for showing me how much I am loved, for taking my stress and anxiety away from me, for all the hope and peace You show me. Lord, I submit to Your ways.

I rebuke any spirit of bad intentions that tries to misguide me. Lord, forgive me of any negative or bad thoughts toward myself or others. Please forgive those whose thoughts are filled with malice or untruths toward me. Free my heart from the chains of revenge or heartache. Fill it instead with Your mercy and love, unconditionally. When I am weak, You are strong.

Lord, I ask that You guide us to Your glory for all we meet and all that we prepare for Your kingdom. Let our words be Your words. Humble us before You to let go of any burdens we are holding on to. In You, we will find wisdom, discernment, and revelation. There's no answer that can't be found in You! It's Your past faithfulness that gives us Yak Hal (hope) for our future.

In Jesus's name, I pray with all my heart and soul.

Amen.

## Dear Lord,

*Thank You for being in my life, for choosing me. Lord, I will lift You up throughout my day. Your will for me is great, powerful, and joyful. Lord, reveal to me my heart and empty all lack of self-control. Replace it with the joy that only comes from knowing You. Let me be joyful throughout my day because You have blessed me with Your presence in everything I do and everyone I meet.*

*Lord, bless each and every daughter who came before You last night. Thank You for bringing us all together. Thank You for giving the courage to those who may have fought with evil spirits to get there. Through You, we all received the profound joy of faith and hope that only comes from You. Thank You, Lord, for loving us so much and choosing us to build Your kingdom. Your Word says that Your mighty power is at work within us. Help us, Lord, to always accomplish more than we can imagine through Your mighty name.*

*In Jesus Christ's name, I pray.*

*Amen.*

## Dear Lord,

I praise You and thank You for all Your great and wonderful promises. Whether in the valleys or on the mountains, Your glory stands. It's Your glory that is forever. Your never leave me. Lord, forgive me for my self-doubts that surface from time to time. Remind me that through You, everything is possible. Remind me that Your love is endless. Help me to understand and believe in Your miracles in my heart every day. I don't need to hide my broken pieces, because it's with those broken pieces of my life that You have constructed Your biggest platform to display Your glory. Lord, grow my relationship with You. I will never be satisfied until I have a full and mature relationship with You, Jesus.

Lord, reveal in me Your strength to show others just how glorious You really are. Lord, bless me with Your favor, grace, and the mercy I need to handle anything today.

In Jesus's name, I pray.

Amen.

## Dear Lord,

*I'm so grateful You chose me! You have given me eyes to see You, ears to hear You, and a compassionate heart to love You. Lord, I am grateful for my family, both related and extended. Please send Your blessings to all of them today. Lord, forgive me for any time I should doubt or have a crisis of belief. Let me take time today to ask for Your wisdom and direction in all that I do. Let me listen to Your voice and have full confidence that You are close and that You will lead me to the good pasture. Thank You for meeting all my needs through Jesus. Give me ears to hear Your voice clearly, to Shema, to not only hear Your words but to obey them always, to have the boldness to follow wherever You call me. I trust and believe that You only have good things in store for me. I will never be outside Your care.*

*Lord, give me an undivided heart to hear You under every circumstance and a pure heart to see You.*

*In Jesus's blessed name, I pray.*

*Amen.*

# Dear Lord,

*Thank You for this day, for all the blessings You have given me and for all the blessings You will give me today. I receive all without reservation. Lord, You are mighty and sovereign. Your words will last forever.*

*Lord, give me strength to be Your disciple of truth, to love those I may not agree with. Infuse true humility into my actions and words, flowing out from my heart of compassion. I offer myself to be molded, surrendering my past hurts, humiliations, and sins to be molded into a likeness of Jesus Christ. Let me emulate the Son, listen to and follow the Holy Spirit, and fear, obey, and love the Father.*

*Lord, forgive anything short of being selfless in my actions and my mind today. And help me to forgive others as You have forgiven me. Fill me only with Your love, wisdom, and grace. Show me to be honest in all my actions, respectful and merciful toward others, whether we agree or not, rebuking every negative thought.*

*Lord, I put Your armor on this morning to remind myself and prepare myself for this day.*

*In the name of Yahweh, our savior and Father.*

*Amen.*

## Dear Lord,

*I admit that I forget that You are with me all the time. I worry about things that are simply out of my control. I often forget what You are like. Please forgive me for forgetting. I want to get to know You better, to know Your Word, to trust in You for everything every day, to not worry about tomorrow or next week but to give all my hope in You today. Help me to put You first in my life. Help me to live one day at a time. Help me not to worry but to focus on what You have for me and what You're doing in my life right now. Let me place my anxieties, my stress, and my worries at Your feet every morning. Lord, I want to trust in Your promise to take care of every one of my needs—financial, relational, physical, social, spiritual, and emotional. Help me, Lord, to trust in You more and worry less.*

*In Jesus's name, I pray.*

*Amen!*

*Cast your cares on the Lord and He will sustain you. (Psalm 55:22 NIV)*

# Dear Lord,

*I know You know me. I know You know my thoughts and my questions about myself, my worries about if I'm worthy of all You can give. Lord, help me to have the kind of faith for Your righteousness in all that I do. That I may see Your glory through me, in all You direct me to do, to let go in all aspects of my life, not just once in a while but in everything, every day. Teach me to be patient with others and kind to those who don't see You. Lord, give me strength in my weaknesses. My fear of failure can be so overwhelming that it sometimes stops me in moving forward and Your good work. Lord, through You I know my life is complete, but when those moments of doubt creep in my mind, and I doubt everything, I need You. The enemy starts filling my head with thoughts that I know aren't true, but they still sneak in. Lord, You created heaven and earth, everything in it, and me. I know You love me, and You gave me all that I need to prevent and rebuke the enemy. Forgive me for these times of unfaithfulness. Give me Your strength to understand and obey. Give me strong faith to believe You will move mountains again and You still perform miracles. Through Your Son, Jesus Christ, all my sins have been forgiven and I am made new in Your eyes every day. By washing in the blood of Christ, I am lifted up to You, Lord. You give me righteousness through Jesus. Through Your love and sacrifice, I am forgiven.*

*In Jesus's name.*

*Amen.*

In You, O Lord, do I put my trust and confidently take refuge; let me never be put to shame or confusion! (Psalm 71:1 NIV)

## Dear Lord,

*Let us feel Your righteousness so we can have peace and faith in all we do and all You ask us to do. We will always stay true to Your Word. You know what's in our hearts before we speak it. Lord, let us put You first in our hearts and help us to put You first in our minds, in our mouths when we speak to You or when we proclaim Your greatness to others. Give us Your grace and wisdom to know when You ask us to speak about Your glory. Let us know when to be quiet in the storms that we encounter, to let You step in and deliver us. Lord, You are our guide through all we do. Please show us the patience we need to slow down, listen to You, and obey in Your time, not our own.*

*In Jesus's name.*

*Amen.*

> Since we have been justified through faith, we have peace with God through our Lord Jesus Christ. (Romans 5:1 NIV)

# Dear Lord,

*Remind me to ask for and to give Your forgiveness throughout my day. Lord, my heart is filed with such joy and gratefulness. I declare that it is all for Your glory. You've blessed my family with Your miracles once again. Thank You, Lord Jesus. Lord, my life on earth is too short to praise and magnify Your name for all You have done for me and my family. Lord, please help me to share Your joy with others who come across my path today. Open their hearts to see You through me and my actions so that they too can experience a joy and a peace that only comes from You. When we open our hearts and accept the Holy Spirit into our lives, when we truly receive the glory of Your power and accept that Jesus died for us, we can see and feel Your grace, love, and peace in our lives.*

*In Jesus's name, I pray.*

*Amen!*

## Dear Lord,

*Show me Your truth. I am before You with an open heart. Teach me to be mindful and to rest at Your feet. Lord, forgive me when I get ahead of myself, thinking I've got it when I really don't. I'm not You. When I listen to You, learn Your Word, and show Your love to others, I know it's what I need to do and You are pleased with me. Lord, forgive me also of my impatience. I know I need to just stop and hand all these things in front of me to You, to let go every day. They are easily defeated by You, and my path becomes clearer. You go before me. You are my rock and my foundation. You are Sovereign, Lord. Lord, teach me to be faithful and righteous in all You want me to do, that when I do it, I give You all the glory and all the victory. I have redemption through You. I have the forgiveness of my sins, and through the blood of Your Son, Jesus Christ, I am given the riches of Your grace.*

*Lord, I will listen, learn, and love.*

*In Jesus's name, I pray.*

*Amen.*

The word of the Lord is right and true; He is faithful in all he does. (Psalm 33:4 NIV)

## Dear Lord,

*Forgive me for any lack of confidence in what You can do in my life at any time. Lord, teach me to pause first, to breathe and ask for You, to stop and listen to Your still, small voice, to have faith so strong that it breeds confidence.*

*Lord, all things are better through You and are lasting in my life. Lord, please bless me with the strength and wisdom of faith that only You can give. Lord, please forgive those who will sin against me today but also bless them with Your mercy. Lord, I know that with everything You've created in this world, You would never forsake us. Lord, lift me up and give me the confidence and faith in times of confusion. Let me know each moment of every crisis that You are who You say You are. You are always on my side. Let my faith in You never waver or ever question Your way. In Your hands, I let go.*

*In Jesus's name, I pray.*

*Amen.*

"You will call upon Me and come and pray to Me, and I will listen to you. You will seek Me and find Me when you seek Me with all your heart." (Jeremiah 29:12–13 NIV)

## Dear Lord,

*I am so thankful to have You in my life, to truly feel Your presence even when You need to correct me. I am thankful for being more and more aware each day as You teach me and test me. I know in my heart that Your love for me outshines any transgressions that I may have. I know that if I just pause long enough, You will show me the way. Forgive me for trying to lead when I should follow. You have so much to give me and show me. Lord, give me the strength to never doubt what You ask me to do. Even if it becomes uncomfortable, let me see the lesson in it. Lord, I celebrate the love and mercy that You give me. I believe You are who You say You are and that You will always do what You say You will do. Lord, guard those who are facing trouble right now. Give them Your grace to face it. Thy will be done on earth as it is in heaven!*

*In Jesus's name, I pray.*

*Amen.*

## Dear Lord,

*Please show me Your love and forgiveness toward others today, even when it's hard for me. Help me to be still and remember all Your grace and sacrifices for us. Let the Holy Spirit show me Your grace and love to forgive. Lord, with the love that You showed us all when You died for our sins, may we remember each day that sacrifice and give to others as You did. Let Your blood wash over us and make us new every day. In You, we are redeemed and Your children. Lord, give us the strength to show others Your glory, to give You all the glory for all our blessings each day. Lord, I pray for the one who is lost, that we can make a difference to them, in Your name.*

*In Jesus's name, I pray.*

*Amen.*

God is working in you, giving you the desire to obey Him and the power to do what pleases Him. (Philippians 2:13 NIV)

# Dear Lord,

*Please bless the lost souls, where evil has influenced them to do harm to innocent angels. Lord, my heart aches for those who are forgotten. I know You have not forgotten them and that they are with You. You have wrapped them in Your love, and they no longer feel the pain. Lord, please let me forgive those who have done the evil on these innocents and to know that Your laws and justice will prevail. Lord, remind me that You are in control and still on the throne. You are the only judge. Lord, bless this beautiful day and thank you for the love You show us every day. Let us not forsake Your love by thinking negatively but embrace the love You have for all of us. Lead us to lean on You first and not on ourselves. We trust Your ways are always better, even when we don't understand them. Lord, we lift up all those who need Your truth and wisdom. Teach us to take in Your Holy Spirit and welcome His directions every day. Lord, give me the strength and wisdom today to forgive.*

*In Jesus Christ's name, I pray.*

*Amen.*

I can do everything through Him who gives me strength. (Philippians 4:13 NIV)

# Dear Lord,

*I'm not perfect, and I struggle every day with what You want me to do. I have to remind myself that even though I think I'm on the right path, it is never my will but Your will that is done. Lord, please always walk with me and show me the patience I need toward others, the grace I need to forgive myself and be mindful of the enemy, to guard my heart at all times. It's so easy to slide into self-gratification of even the simple things. Lord, quiet my thoughts that try to run rampant and guide me back to You and what You have for me. Lord, thank You for the blessings in my life. Teach me to always be humble, to reflect on the words that want to come out my mouth, to stop and give You the glory always. Lord, let my thoughts not lead to boasting or self-righteousness, declaring Your good deeds, but to know You, and only You should see them. My heart is open to Your Holy Spirit. I am Your servant, excited for what You can do through me. Lord, give me strength to remember You every moment of every day and open more space for Your pleasing will.*

*In Jesus's name, I pray.*

*Amen.*

Create in me a pure heart, O God and renew a steadfast spirit within me. (Psalm 51:10 NIV)

## Dear Lord,

*Bless those who have forgotten to receive Your love and prayers. Lord, You give me strength each day. You give me Your daily bread. Let me always pause to accept Your grace and believe that all things are possible through You. Humans do not have any control. It is only the enemy who makes us think so. It's the enemy who causes us to be boastful and prideful. Lord, I know I have Your love, that I am free from all my sins, that I can be happy with the humbleness You give me, that I can have peace, because any doubt of who I Am is stops at Your feet. The Holy Spirit fills my soul with Your light and blessings. I accept what Jesus did for me. I know I am a child of God!*

*In Jesus's name, I pray.*

*Amen.*

If anyone is in Christ, he is a new creation; the old has gone, the new has come! (2 Corinthians 5:17 NIV)

# Dear Lord,

*Thank You for Your constant direction, showing Your plans for me. Forgive me for not seeing them immediately. The enemy tries to run in front of those plans, but the enemy isn't welcome here! Lord, it's so easy every day, with the normal trials and constant distractions, to not see through all the confusion. Lord, grant me the wisdom to pause and ponder, to not react.*

*Lord, please bless those who are hurting and broken and need Your message, a word from You. They long to know they are loved. Show them that they are worthy of all You have to give them, that they can be redeemed. Show them Your grace of forgiveness and how comforting it is to let go and open their hearts completely to the Holy Spirit. Lord, teach us to become Your disciples and to wait patiently for Your instructions, however small they may seem. Let us reach out to those who are broken. We lift them up to You. They need You. They need to realize they are at the end of themselves and are ready to submit to Your will. Nothing You have for us will ever put us to shame, only what we try to do without You. We are all the same in Your eyes. All You ask is for us to keep Your Word, live Your Word, and love You with all our hearts, minds, and souls.*

*In Jesus Christ, we surrender.*

*Amen.*

In You, O Lord, do I put my trust and confidently take refuge; let me never be put to shame or confusion! (Psalm 71:11 NIV)

## Dear Lord,

*Please open my heart before my mouth. Show me to always pause and ponder before I act, think, or say something.*

*Lord, this morning, I can feel Your love and strength building in me and around me. I can feel Your angel armies gathering in our sights, not just for our protection but to go before us and battle unforeseen enemies. I am not scared, Lord, but I feel excited to be with You. Lord, every day, You give us Your grace and mercy to be bold, to be truthful in the Word, to minister and give hope to those who need to believe in You. Lord, bless those who are hurting and confused. Please let them know Your goodness. The dark can be too easy at times. Tear the darkness that holds them and give them the light. Let me be Your hands and feet to show them Your warmth and love. That is where Your children belong and where You want them all to be to receive Your glory and the power.*

*I declare that the angel armies will defeat all the enemies that are trying to stifle the good and the light!*

*In Jesus's name.*

*Amen.*

Be strong and courageous. The Lord your God will be
with you wherever you go. (Joshua 1:9 NIV)

# Dear Lord,

*Let us all go forward today with forgiveness and love in our hearts. I call on Archangel Michael to go before us and protect us as we show Your mercy with grace and wisdom. Give us the confidence and courage to step out in light, to show others Your light is stronger than the darkness in this world. Lord, help us to use the specific gifts and talents that each of us possess, to be seen and used in Your name. Lord, let us have Your eyes today to see those who are hurting. Let us have Your wisdom to speak honor and glory over them in Your name, Lord. You are our great healer. Thank You for Your blessings on us all. We deny ourselves and walk with You, only in Your will.*

*In Jesus's name, I pray.*

*Amen.*

Be strong in the Lord and in his mighty power. Put on the full armor of God, so you can take a stand against the devils schemes. (Ephesians 6:10–11 NIV)

## Dear Lord,

*Thank You for Your love and forgiveness of my sins today. As I pray, open my heart to Your Word. Don't let me trip on my own words and thoughts. Lord, send me Your grace and mercy to deal with the tests and situations You put in my path, to never forget Your glory, and to never give up hope, even when the sun isn't shining. Hope is what will deliver me to Your grace. Lord, I know I have to remember and rekindle my focus and faith in You every morning. You are what's right and true. With Your love, I can do anything through You. Lord, please take all my worries and concerns that I place at Your feet. Let me relax and just be Your hands and feet today, to walk in Your wishes for me, not my own selfish thoughts. Thy will be done.*

*In Jesus's name.*

*Amen.*

# Dear Lord,

*I know You are not the author of stress and anxiety. I struggle with letting that creep into my mind when I know I should let go of it. The enemy loves to see me wrestle with worry rather than hand it over to You. He loves to pick at the embers and make it a fire. But, Lord, I trust in You. I rebuke all the wrong and deceitful tricks Satan tries on me and my mind. I know in my heart that the enemy would only keep trying if he was afraid—because my love for You, Lord, gets stronger and stronger each day. Your love for me is always worth my obedience as I hand You my worries and concerns. Your blessings are far and above what I deserve. Give me strength today, Lord, to let go of all the negative thoughts, all the false concerns, and trust in You. You will not forsake me. You have chosen me to be Your light in the darkness of the world. Lord, I banish the enemy from my mind today. Let me shine for others. Let me continue to live humbly through You, through Your love.*

*In Jesus's name, I pray.*

*Amen.*

Live a life of love, just as Christ loved us and gave Himself up for us as a fragrant offering and sacrifice to God. (Ephesians 5:2 NIV)

## Dear Lord,

*Forgive us of our thoughts of disappointment and anger toward others. We know You have a plan. Lord, forgive those who have and will sin against us. Let there only be truth in the words. No matter what the circumstance or the outcome of any situation, our commitment is to You, and we will always give You the glory, no matter what. In Your glory, we thrive. Please help us to be at peace in times of confusion and strife. Lord, Your words can be so encouraging to us, if we just listen, so let us seek You for the answers, not ourselves. Lord, please lift up those who are hurting or confused. Let Your Holy Spirit surround their souls and let them feel Your peace. Help us and give us strength in wisdom and grace to understand we aren't in control, but with our trust in You, we can let go and let You be in control. You fight our battles and answer our prayers. Open our eyes and hearts to Your Word today. Please bless all the lost souls. Give us Your eyes to find the one and deliver Your Word so that they know You are our living God.*

*In Jesus's name, I pray.*

*Amen.*

# Dear Lord,

*Thank You for giving us another beautiful day, another day to get it right. Lord, I ask for Your mercy when I don't get it right. Your grace has been given to me in spite of not being perfect. Lord, You bless us with kindness and goodness. All You ask of us is to take Your good news to others, to help them see they are also children of God, no matter what. Lord, I give You all the glory for the gifts You have given me and shown me. Without You, I am nothing, and my soul would not feel. In this world, we ask to be Your servants, Lord, to be faithful to You and to be merciful to others. God, please bless those hurting and confused. You can heal. You are the light in their darkness. Lord, grant me an open heart, open ears, and a quiet mouth today so I can hear Your Holy Spirit.*

*In Jesus's name, I pray.*

*Amen,*

> I will exalt you Lord for you lifted me out of the depths and did not let my enemies float over me. (Psalm 30:1 NIV)

# *Dear Lord,*

*Why is it so hard to let go? We think that we can do it all, that we can fix it. It becomes so easy to be anxious over things that are never in our control. The more I try to fix it, the more distant it becomes. It's like chasing something and never catching it. Lord, I hand it all over to You. My faith is strong in You and all that You can do. I know that with faith and prayer, You will never shame me. Lord, I ask that You take away all the worry and pain in my heart. Take away the struggle and turn it to hope. Your ways, Lord, are higher than my ways, and Your thoughts are greater than my thoughts. Lord, please deliver those who are lost from the enemy that keeps torturing them. Let my struggle not be in vain but give me hope in You, Lord. I know You always hear me because I see Your glory and blessings every day in my life. Please bless the lost and bring them home.*

*In Jesus's name, I pray.*

*Amen.*

> Therefore since we have been justified through faith, we have peace with God through our Lord Jesus Christ. (Romans 5:1 NIV)

## Dear Lord,

*Please forgive me for the times I hold back and try to handle things on my own. My stubbornness is my downfall. Lord, You are my living God. You love all of us. We can still be tricked by the enemy to act and make decisions without You. Lord, give me Your grace today to be still and listen. It's Your love and understanding that will guide me through. Lord, I open my heart and my soul to Your Holy Spirit, to fill me and guide me, all in the name of Jesus Christ. Lord, He lives in me, and I in Him. Let me show others Your mercy and love today. Teach me to leave frustration and stubbornness at the curb for the trash to be taken away. I know it has no place in my life or for Your victory. I am a victor through You, never a victim!*

*In Jesus Christ, I pray.*

*Amen.*

## Dear Lord,

*I ask You for Your grace and love today, for Your guidance. See through my hardness of heart, my thick headedness, my stubborn ways, and my selfish passions. All of them keep me from truly knowing You. Lord, please let me release my daily worries and fears to You. You tell me, "Be not afraid, for I Am with you." I know You are our Sovereign Lord, and I shouldn't be afraid. I know that Your love for me is endless. Lord, I forget this truth sometimes, and I let the enemy tell me that I'm alone. I know that's a lie. I know that through You and with You, all things are possible. Lord, I trust You to direct my steps on the right path. You only see good for me. There is no place on my path for fear or worry. Lord, give me the strength to release all my worries to You.*

*In Jesus's name, I pray.*

*Amen.*

## Dear Lord,

*As I pray with You this morning, I hear You tell me that I am forgiven and that so many others can be forgiven through Your love, to trust You and believe You are always there every step of the way. Forgive me of my sins. I don't easily let go of my cares and worries. It's something I was taught to do through life. "Hang on to them and fix it. Own them and make it happen." But as I've come to know You, I am learning that I might as well be running in place if I think that to be truth. My control of anything gets me nowhere. Lord, I trust You today with all my cares and worries. To You, I will remain faithful, and I will obey Your direction for me. Lord, release Your Holy Spirit in me today. Let me be an example of Your love to others.*

*In Jesus's name, I pray.*

*Amen.*

Cast your cares on the Lord and he will sustain you;
He will never let the Righteous be shaken. (Psalm
55:22 NIV)

## Dear Lord,

*Thank You for this beautiful day, another day to walk in Your Word, to try to be better and more obedient. Lord, give me a heart like Mary's. She never doubted what You told her to do. She obeyed Your direction for her. She didn't try to back out or rationalize what You gave her, even though it meant facing a sure death. You have a plan for each of us. That plan will have its challenges, its ups and downs, its happiness and its sadness, but no matter what, Your plan is the best for us. Lord, please help my soul to be totally open and receptive to Your plan. Don't let my pride get in the way. Transform me to Your way and to the obedience I need to follow, even if sometimes it doesn't make sense to me. Lord, give me Your grace to deliver all to You. For God's glory and in Jesus's name.*

*Amen.*

## Dear Lord,

*Please give me Your grace to be silent when I am faced with a circumstance or person I may not agree with, or someone who I feel has been rude or unkind. I know I should be silent, that You will fight my battles. You will weigh all things, and it's never my place to find justice or to find fault. Holy Spirit, let me see through the chaos and be at peace, to believe, to know that with You and in You, all is right. Through Your eyes, I will become righteous. What You think of me matters most to me. Lord, I pray that today I can let go of things. After all, they are really small and trivial. Only love comes from my heart.*

*In Jesus's name, I pray.*

*Amen.*

# Dear Lord,

*Thank You for giving me this beautiful day, another day to learn and be closer to You. Help me today, Lord, to be more like You, and by Your grace and mercy in my heart, to let go of my worries and stress. Please stand in the way of me. Don't let me take control of things that are already out of my control. I know that is my weakness and a sin of not fully trusting You with all my heart. Lord, it's so hard to admit that I can still sin against You with this lack of trust. I know I have so much more to learn and accept. Lord, help me to remove my pride and my own self-centeredness and give all the control to You. I know that what You have for me is good. Grant me Your grace through the Holy Spirit to acknowledge it and hand it all over, even when my flesh wants the power of control.*

*Lord, I want my heart to serve You before myself. I want words that flow from a heart that loves others more than myself.*

*In Jesus's name, I pray.*

*Amen.*

> For it is by grace you have been saved, through faith-and this is not from yourselves, it is the gift of God-not by works, so that no one can boast. (Ephesians 2:8 NIV)

# Dear Lord,

*Bless this beautiful day. Please bless those I meet today and those I meet who are in need. Please give me the right words to lift them and declare Your mercy and love on their hearts.*

*Lord, all that You give to me makes me stronger. Fill me with the grace and wisdom to meet the tests and the challenges that I face. Lord, Your love for me tells me that You have all my worries and concerns. Your goodness follows me, and I know that if I would just stop once in a while and fix my eyes on You, everything will become clear. I can do everything through You. And in my weaknesses, You are strong. You alone can fight my battle and right my wrongs. You can lift me up to Your higher place. But I have to have the patience and faith strong enough to believe. Lord, I need Your patience to wait on You. I rebuke the enemy and the lies he tries to tell me. He has no control over me. Lord, help me be distracted from myself and see the need that others may have to see where You are at work today and help You.*

*Lord, You are my healer and provider for all things.*

*In Jesus's name, I pray.*

*Amen.*

## Dear Lord,

*Thank You for all Your blessings. You see what we need, however big or small, and You deliver it to us. You fill my heart with so much joy and thankfulness for Your gifts. Every blessing that You give us is a miracle. Lord, teach me to always be grateful to You, to have thanksgiving and praise You always, even when times get tough. This is Your will for my life. Lord, break the power of the enemy in my life. Defeat him through my obedience and praise to You. Change my attitude at all times to one of joyful contentment, no matter what my circumstances are. I thank You for all the blessings yet to come in my life through Your promises to me. Give me Your attitude of humility and thankful acceptance, to learn contentment in every circumstance I'm in, to always praise You. Teach me to have a thankful heart. I know that Your truth dwells in a thankful heart.*

*In Jesus's name, I pray.*

*Amen.*

> Whoever believes in Him is not condemned, but whoever does not believe stands condemned already because they have not believed in the name of God's one and only Son. (John 3:18 NIV)

## Dear Lord,

*Please grant me grace and patience to forgive those who will sin against me and test me today.*

*Lord, let me rest in Your presence and let go of things I try to control. Give me the faith I need to believe that You are in control. By the Holy Spirit that lives in me, I know Your will is greater than mine. It's in those times of doubt I ask for strength to dismiss and rebuke the enemy and his petty thoughts. Be. Not. Afraid. Give me the faith as big as a mustard seed so I can see You move the mountains before me. Lord, I give You my life for Your plans.*

*In Jesus's name, I pray.*

*Amen.*

## Dear Lord,

*Please grant me Your grace and wisdom. Let my heart open to the Holy Spirit and give me the faith and commitment I need for this journey. Lord, there have been bumps and snags, but You have always set me right. You've given me Your blessings. Lord, through Your grace and wisdom, I can be at peace. Discipline me to be humble and to give all the glory to You, Lord.*

*Lord, I am letting go of all that binds up in my head, and I am releasing all my worries to You. Only peace will guide me today.*

*Jesus, in Your powerful name, I pray.*

*Amen.*

## Dear Lord,

*Forgive me for not having the faith in You and in everything You have planned for me. Lord, I know that when I have doubts or worries, I am sinning against You. Lord, I give all my concerns of my inequities, all my transgressions of thought to You. It's for You to decide, not me. I know sometimes I can feel so overwhelmed, but please teach me to pause more often at these moments and to release all control to You. Lord, please give me Your mercy, grace, and wisdom to defeat these thoughts. Teach me to be more obedient to Your Word and promises. With You, I have nothing to fear. In You, I am not afraid. Lead me to Your quiet and still places.*

*I declare that right now blessings are pouring over me!*

*I declare I will fulfill my destiny, in Your name and all for Your glory!*

*Jesus, I pray this in Your name.*

*Amen.*

## Dear Lord,

*Thank You this day for all the blessings in my life, for the grace and wisdom You give me. Lord, please give me strength to rebuke the enemy, to not believe the lies he tries to tell me. I know, Lord, that You go before me every day to fight my battles. And through Your righteousness and grace, I can lay all my worries or concerns at Your feet. You are Sovereign, Lord. All that is good shines through You to me. Lord, thank You for the presence of Your Holy Spirit, who guides me daily. Even though I may go off thinking, I have this, You remind me that I don't through Your Spirit. Lord, I step out in faith today with Your belt of truth, Your breastplate of righteousness, Your shield of faith, Your helmet of my salvation, and Your sword of the Holy Spirit and Your Word. Lord, let me be the light and show love and grace to the one. Jesus, in Your powerful and precious name, I pray for peace to be with our group tonight. I declare that peace and love will be all that people see. I declare that Your angel armies surround us. I declare all things through You, Jesus!*

*In Jesus's name, I pray.*

*Amen.*

> Blessed is the one, whose transgressions are forgiven whose sins are covered. Blessed is the one, whose sin the Lord does not count against them and in whose spirit is no deceit. (Psalm 32:1–2 NIV)

# Dear Lord,

*Forgive me when the faith in myself becomes greater than my faith in You. Let me learn like Elijah and become faithful in You with no questions, even when I don't see a way. Let it be automatic. Your ways are far more superior than what I see before me. Lord, forgive me for putting limits on my life. You are my redeemer, my restorer of everything. You knew me before I was born. Please give me Your wisdom and grace to always believe that. Never doubt it. Your mercy is my gift. By You, I am completely forgiven and blessed. And through You, I am declared perfectly righteous. I am priceless and worthy because of the sacrifice You gave me. Let me lay down my worries and follow You. I know You have me in Your hands, no matter what. Every day, You fight to bring me closer to You. Lord, I lay it all at Your feet today. I will not struggle. I declare the Lord's prosperity in my life today!*

*In Jesus's name, I pray.*

*Amen.*

Let it be known today that you are God in Israel and that I am your servant. (1 King 18:36 NIV)

# Dear Lord,

*Please forgive me of my transgressions of impatience. Lord, bless and forgive those who sin against me. Lord, here I am with You this morning. Lord, let me be patient today and give up everything I can't control. Please take any fear of failure away. Help me to see that it is what You think of me that ultimately matters. You know me, and You know what is in front of me. If I would just stop and listen to Your Holy Spirit, I would understand that You have it all.*

*Lord, grant me Your grace to deal with all the enemy tries to send my way. His lies won't prosper in my mind. I declare to You, Lord, that with You by my side, anything can be overcome. Thank You for the beautiful day. Thank You for the mercy You show me, for all the blessings You have given me and will give me. Your love is overwhelming and has filled my heart. In Your name and for Your glory, I will show others Your love today, because of Your belief in me and what You want me to do, to let others know You are still on the throne. You are our Sovereign Lord!*

*In Jesus's name, I pray.*

*Amen.*

> Trust in the Lord with all your heart and lean not on your own understanding; in all your ways submit to him and he will make your paths straight. (Proverbs 3:5 NIV)

# Dear Lord,

I want to be more like You every day, to fulfill the things You want me to do. But I hit walls and obstacles that challenge that. I know in all my heart that as long as I keep my eyes fixed on You, I won't stumble. Lord, give me the strength of hope and faith to see all the possibilities You have for me. There are always miracles that happen. Open my eyes to them. Lord, please bless those in my life who are struggling with the belief that You are our creator and provider, and bless those in my life who You have brought to me and who love You as much as I do. Thank You for that continual contact with like brothers and sisters who believe in You. It recharges me every day. Lord, thank You for Your abundant gifts. "My cup runneth over."

Lord, I love You with all my heart, all my mind, and all my soul, wholly.

In Jesus's name, I pray.

Amen.

> Depend on the Lord in whatever you do, and your plans will succeed. (Proverbs 16:3 NIV)

## Dear Lord,

Thank You for this beautiful day, for all the days You are in my life! Lord, forgive me of my sins. Forgive me when I feel shame or question what someone says or their motives. Lord, You are my rock, my foundation. I stand firm on the rock and give thanks to You! You see everything in my heart, and I know that those thoughts of insignificance or self-doubt are thoughts the enemy tries to put in my head. But the enemy can't touch my heart. My heart belongs to You. Let the Holy Spirit mold me to what You want me to be. Give me the wisdom to know better. Lord, thank You for hearing me, for believing in me, no matter what. I only care what You think of me. I am Your child, and I will walk in Your presence. Lord, please open the hearts of those around me so that they can also experience Your love and grace.

In Jesus's name, I pray.

## Dear Lord,

*Forgive me for being afraid of what I think I lack. Lord, I know You believe in me. Lord, let me believe in myself as much as You do. Show me how to forgive myself for things that are long past, decisions made that are long past. Lord, I ask for strength and mercy to forgive others, to let the Holy Spirit's wisdom guide me through all my hills and valleys. Clean my heart and show me what I need to see to let go, to stand up and carry my cross to follow You. Lord, I know that when I'm stuck with these bitter and hurtful feelings, my reactions don't help me. They are not for Your name. I lay all these thoughts of unforgiveness at Your feet. I do not own them anymore. Lord, I will forgive others right here, right now, as You have forgiven me. I will also forgive myself in Your precious name. I will not give strength to other people's opinions and judgments. It's only You, Lord, that I care to impress. Teach me to be humble, loving, and faithful through every day and everything, to trust in You, Lord, no matter what.*

*In Jesus's name, I pray.*

*Amen.*

## Dear Lord,

*I praise You! You are my rock! You are my way, my truth, and my life! Lord, I know it's so easy to give You glory and thanks when everything is going well. And it's always so hard to praise You and to be thankful during the quiet seasons or the seasons of testing. Lord, I give You all the glory for the love You show me, for Your wisdom that directs my steps throughout my day, and for Your grace and mercy toward my transgressions. Holy Spirit, continue to be in me. Never leave me to my own will but to trust in Your will. Lord, thank You for the answers to my questions. They are proof that You are still on the throne and still in control. I rebuke all evil and temptations that try to get in my way. There is no place for them before me. There is no reason for me to ever be afraid. You are my savior and my redeemer.*

*In Jesus's glorious name, I pray.*

*Amen.*

> May your unfailing love come to me lord, your salvation, according to your promise; then I can answer anyone who haunts me, for I trust in your word. (Psalms 119:41 NIV)

# Dear Lord,

You are our great God! Our only God! You give us such wonderful blessings. No one will ever go before You. Lord, give us the wisdom You want us to have so we can open our eyes to see You at work. Let us be patient and wait for You. It's so easy to rush to solve things, but in our hurry, we miss Your blessings on us. Lord, please forgive us of our impatience. Teach us to love one another, even when it's most difficult. Search our hearts and release any feelings of hurt or evil. May the Holy Spirit guide us to make the right decisions in how we act every day with others. Get rid of any pride that traps us and uses us against Your will. Guide us, Lord.

In Jesus's name, I pray.

Amen.

## Dear Lord,

*Thank You for Your blessings. Forgive me of my shallow sins. Thank You for the grace that You show me. Let me walk in obedience in Your light and always give You the glory of my blessings. Lord, even when my world is dark and I walk in the valley of death, I know You are beside me. I praise You and worship only You for the blessings You have given and will give me. I am grateful for the opportunity to be closer to You. Lord, please give me the strength and the wisdom I will need today to fix my eyes on You, through all that is before me. Your will be done.*

*Lord, please bless the one who is lost. Bring them back to the ninety-nine. Remove the covers from their eyes.*

*In Jesus's name, I pray.*

*Amen!*

Observe the commands of the Lord your God, walking in obedience to him and revering him. (Deuteronomy 8:6 NIV)

# Dear Lord,

*You are my redeemer. Thank You for always being near and for blessing me. Lord, forgive me when I get frustrated and confused as to what I should do. Forgive me when I get angry over things I can't control. Lord, my sinful nature goes automatically to those thoughts of self-reliance and control. And I know those thoughts don't align with You and Your will. Lord, give me Your wisdom that You teach, and the grace to accept it, even if it's not what I think the answer should be. Lord, I am grateful for the cross, for all that was sacrificed for me, for the power of the sacrifice that Your Son, Jesus Christ, did for us. I am forgiven each morning. Lord, give me the strength today to obey Your Word, to love rather than to immediately judge others. Lord, I put my life in Your hands. Mold me and humble me in Your righteousness.*

*In Jesus's name, I pray.*

*Amen.*

# Dear Lord,

*Forgive my fear and doubt. Lord, You are my savior, the One and only. Your Holy Spirit is in me by Your grace. Your goodness, mercy, and graciousness have been given to me through Your Son. I rebuke any temptation to not believe that You are in control. Let me see You more as You want to be seen. Everything I see is about You. I don't deserve it, but You still give me Your grace and love through everything that I face. Your goodness, Your patience, and Your love are for me. Lord, the Spirit that resides in me gives me the faith in all things. It's not about talking about it but believing it and moving through it. Let me show hope to others today, and teach me to be better through You. I want to please You, to be Your hands and feet in this world today. So take my weaknesses away and give me Your strength and power to stand against all fear when the enemy tries to block my path.*

*In Jesus's powerful name.*

*Amen.*

## Dear Lord,

*Some are still blind to Your glory and goodness. Lord, open my heart to receive You today. Keep it open so I don't miss anything. Your blessings are abundant. Thank You for Your grace. Your grace stays patient with me as I walk through my hills and valleys. Lord, thank You for Your mercy. Sometimes I don't think I deserve it, but Your mercy is always there. Its patience is an example to me of how I should be to others, to show the mercy rather than judgment to others. Thank You for the peace You always offer so freely when I trust in You and not my stubbornness. Lord, give to me and my loved ones abundantly all Your blessings, to have grace mercy and peace as You do. Teach me to be patient and to rest in the peace, instead of joining the craziness of the masses. Teach me to pause and breathe in Your words, to listen for and hear Your still, small voice. I push my pride away, so I can hear You today.*

*In Jesus's victorious name.*

*Amen!*

The grace of our Lord was poured out on me abundantly, along with the faith and love that are in Jesus Christ. (1 Timothy 1:14 NIV)

# Dear Lord,

*Help me to accept myself as I am. Help me see what You see. The bad thoughts I can have make me feel small, resentful, scared, and unworthy of Your love, which makes me unable to love others and love You as I should. Help me, Lord, to never compromise my integrity to win favor, but to be authentic, truthful, and honest in everything. And may I never again need to reject myself or sabotage my own happiness and confidence. I can resist criticizing myself. I am beautifully and wonderfully made in Your image. Let the power of Your love be present in my whole being, that I may see myself and everyone through the eyes of Your love. Help me no longer live my life according to what I think others want but by Your will.*

*Lord, I know You are always with me. Open my eyes in times of stress and anxiety, that I may fix my eyes on You and be at peace.*

*In Jesus's name, I pray.*

*Amen.*

## Dear Lord,

Thank You for Your blessings, for the faith, hope, and love You give me, reminding me of whose I am.

Lord, give me Your strength to stand against the darkness that tries to stop me and control my thoughts. You said, "Everything with God," and. Lord, I know I am blessed through Your sacrifice, through You and Your love for me. Lord, let me have the faith I need to push away any doubts and let go. It's Your will. Let me be Your hands and feet today, pulling my strength and hope from You.

In Jesus's name, I pray.

Amen.

# Dear Lord,

*Bless those around me and open my heart and mind to love them, to see their strengths and beauty, not their weaknesses, to trust in You, Lord, to guide me to Your victory. Let me be mindful of the thoughts that can try to destroy Your victory, to rebuke the enemy, who is negative and replace it with Your words of faith and wisdom. Lord, do not let my tongue drive me and control my heart. Lord, I know that with my faith in You, I can eliminate any doubt. I need to trust that faith. And, Lord, with Your righteousness, I can defeat any enemy that tries to defeat me. Lord, I pray for my eyes to be opened, for my heart to be pruned and opened to Your Holy Spirit that lives in me, to receive it and worship it today and break all that binds me.*

*Lord, in Jesus's powerful name.*

*Amen.*

Since we have been justified through faith, we have peace with God through our Lord Jesus Christ. (Romans 5:1 NIV)

## Dear Lord,

*Thank You for the blessings You give me every day, for the peace and mercy You show me. Lord, I know You are with me through all things. I know I am Your beloved. Even when You are silent, I can feel You with me, and my heart is content. Lord, Your Holy Spirit gives me strength to do whatever You ask me to do. And Your glory is shown in all the things You help me do. Please give me Your grace and wisdom to show those in my life that they need You too. Open their hearts to see You so their ways are Your ways, not their own.*

*Lord, bless those who are lost and need You so desperately. Let me be Your light today for them. Let me show the hope they can have when they trust in You. Let it not just be words through my mouth but nourishment to their bodies and their souls. Let them breathe in Your words and feel the goodness and the warmth. Let them know that they can do anything with You as their foundation. Let us praise You and Your goodness in all things. Let us welcome the Holy Spirit and the power He gives us.*

*In Jesus Christ, I pray.*

*Amen.*

## Dear Lord,

*You are my light and my warmth. You calm the storms inside of us. You teach us how to show grace and mercy to the lost.*

*Lord, I know You always go before us, and You will go before us tonight. It's You who fights the battles and splits the seas. It's You who delivers us from the evil one. We have nothing to fear with You in our presence, surrounding us, filling us. We praise You, Lord, for all the blessings that You have shown us and will show us and for all the promises You have given us!*

*Lord, we are Your hands and feet today, to show the lost that they are not cold or forsaken, but they can also find warmth in Your love. Let Your fire in us consume them. Your mercy and love are endless. Lord, You have shown me all of it, and I will be Your messenger, Your servant.*

*I praise You! All this, Lord, is for and in Your glory!*

*I declare Your angel armies have surrounded each of us and have protected us while the Holy Spirit works through us this day.*

*In Jesus Christ's powerful name.*

*Amen.*

## Dear Lord,

*Thank You for Your forgiveness through Your Son, Jesus Christ.*

*Thank You for the blessings You have given me and Your promises yet to come.*

*Lord, Your Spirit lives in me to show me what pleases You. Lord, guide me to rely on Your good and wonderful will rather than immediately making a decision on my own. Send me the patience to wait for You, to die each morning and be renewed by Your love. Lord, give me Your grace and mercy to let go of all things I want to control or worry about, placing them at Your feet instead—all of them, no matter the fear the enemy tries to send.*

*I trust in You, Jesus. You are my savior and light.*

*In Jesus's name, I pray.*

*Amen.*

> So, my brothers and sisters, you also died to the law through the body of Christ, that you might belong to another, to Him who was raised from the dead, in order for we may beat fruit for God. (Romans 7:14 NIV)

# Dear Lord,

*Show me Your Holy Spirit. Let him open my heart and invade my mind. Stir up Your fullness of the Holy Spirit in me. Help me grow in my relationship with Him. Help me, Lord, to remember I don't know everything and to be OK with that. Fill me with the Holy Spirit so I understand everything You tell me and what is happening in my life. Lord, open my mind to understand Your truths and to have faith when I cannot see. Lord, open my heart to receive Your blessings and promises, to receive Your good seed and to grow and produce Your fruit for others.*

*Lord, give me the hope and faith I need filled every day, so I don't worry about things I can't see before me. Help me to put all my trust in You, to believe deep in my heart that Your plan for me is much higher than I could ever see for myself. Lord, I ask for the Holy Spirit in me to guide me today.*

*In Jesus's name, I pray.*

*Amen.*

# Dear Lord,

Bless all whose transgressions are forgiven, as Your Word says. And bless those whose sins are not counted against them.

Lord, thank You for the Holy Spirit in my heart that guides me each day. I don't always hear the directions because of all the daily noise and distractions in my head. Teach me to stop and quiet the noise, to slow down and listen to You, to know that all that I do isn't for my glory but for Your glory. Lord, my heart aches when I don't stop and give You time to speak to me. I get too busy with other things. My mind questions who I am to You. But just as soon as the lies appear in my head, You rescue me and speak to me. You reveal Your message to me. And it's always on target. Lord, my heart is faithful. Please give my mind the wisdom to follow my heart. I stand by Your Word and Your promises. I'm excited to be patient in anticipation of Your Word and what You call me to do. In my heart, I can feel You. Grant my mind the patience to wait for You.

In Jesus Christ, my redeemer.

Amen.

## Dear Lord,

*I pray this morning to empty myself, to leave every space open to be filled by Your Holy Spirit. Teach me how to consistently do that each morning so I can stand against all the enemy's schemes to scare me. Teach me to bear the fruit of the Holy Spirit through my thoughts and actions, to have joy, love, knowledge, peace, long-suffering, and humility, to be gentle and show kindness. I ask this not only for my own Spirit but to show those around me the Spirit through Your Word. I lay down all of myself and ask for the Holy Spirit to guide me today. I'm anxious and eager to receive Your work in me, to revive the gifts of the Holy Spirit that already live in me. Lord, grant me the faith to always know that the Holy Spirit lives in me and has never forsaken me.*

*I'm the name of Jesus Christ, I pray.*

*Amen.*

# Dear Lord,

*Thank You for this beautiful day!*

*Lord, give me the grace to see Your blessings, the wisdom to hear Your blessings, and the love to show others Your blessings. You are the one who gives us the strength each day to deliver our fears and worries at Your feet.*

*Lord, I am so thankful for my renewed relationship with You. I'm excited for what lies ahead. To be able to spend more time with You every day is a blessing. I am grateful.*

*Lord, please guard the ones I pray for. Give them strength and perseverance to find Your hope, the hope that lies in each of us, to listen to Your Holy Spirit for Your directions, and to feel the hope and not listen to the lies the enemy tries to confuse us with. Lord, Your way is worthy of each of us. Let us dwell near You and follow You with love and peace in our hearts.*

*In Jesus's powerful name.*

*Amen.*

> In You, O Lord, do I put my trust and confidently take refuge; let me never be put to shame or confusion! (Psalm 71:1 NIV)

## Dear Lord,

*I know it's Your Word that saves me. I know that You have nothing but good things for me. I am excited for what You want me to do. Lord, give me Your grace to accept Your mercy and to be humble before You, to put others before my own thoughts. When the enemy tries to get in my head and make me worry and stress, let me turn to the power of Your name to rebuke the enemy and humble myself before You, not listening to the lies but turning to You, trusting only in You. Give me humility like Jesus to serve others before myself. Lord, I declare I am obedient in Your Word today. There is no other. With my mind and tongue, I will always acknowledge Your power and Your glory!*

*Forever and ever!*

*In Jesus Christ's name.*

*Amen.*

# Dear Lord,

*Show me how to forgive those who will sin against me.*

*Lord, help me to be more Christlike, to turn to You in times of need or doubt rather than leaning on my own decisions. Lord, keep me in Your sight so that I will always stay pointed toward You. Keep my heart excited to continue my journey, as if I was running the race for the ultimate prize. Do not let me get tripped up by what the enemy tries to tell me or throw my way. Lord, every morning, I ask for You to forgive me and renew my mind in You. All the victories of my day are for Your glory! I am eternally thankful.*

*In Jesus's name.*

*Amen.*

> For it is we who are the circumcision, we who serve God by His Spirit, who boast in Christ Jesus, and who put no confidence in the flesh. (Philippians 3:3)

# Dear Lord,

Thank You for this beautiful day. On this day, let us rejoice in You, Lord. Let us truly show our gentleness so others can see. We know You are near. Let us have love, joy, and peace toward others, no matter the circumstance. Today, we can all be still and listen to our Lord and Savior. There is no reason for me to be anxious about anything. The Lord provides for all of us if we will let him. Lord, I praise You! In all Your glory! I am thankful for all You have shown me and taught me and given me, not just this last year but throughout my life. You have brought me to a place of peace with You. Let us celebrate You today and every day!

In Jesus's name, I pray.

Amen!

Spiritual blessings are based on the work of the Trinity:

1. Selection of the Father
2. Sacrifice of the Son
3. Seal of the Holy Spirit

Spiritual blessings begin with and are based on the election to God. He chose You!

Salvation is God's doing, not ours.

Though it is an act of grace, based on His will, a person is responsible for believing.

Thus, God chose You to be saved through belief in the truth.

## Dear Lord,

Renew my mind this morning. Let my mind be a holy sacrifice to Your good and pleasing will. Lord, forgive me of my sins and please forgive those who will sin against me. Lord, fill me with Your Holy Spirit and refresh me. Give me Your mercy and grace to see through Your eyes, to see where there is need. Lord, Your grace is enough. Please bind any fears and anxieties so that through You I can see and feel the hope that lies in front of me. Let me throw away all the lies so that I can see the truth today. Give me the patience to see what is right in front of me, instead of looking behind me or too far in front of me. It's the here and now that matters to You.

Lord, You are the great I Am.

Through You, all things are possible!

In Jesus's name, I pray.

Amen!

# Dear Lord,

*I'm always so amazed at Your forgiveness and Your grace. I have to continue to remind myself that Your Spirit lives in me. The depth and width of Your love for me cannot be understood. Even though the enemy tries to tell me that I'm on my own, You truly are cheering me on, not waiting for me to make a mistake or fail so You can catch me. You are always here for me, Lord. No matter what, You will always love me.*

*Lord, give me Your grace and wisdom today to slow down and wait for Your direction. I invite Your Holy Spirit into my heart to direct my steps today. Fill my heart with understanding and compassion for things I may not know. Never let me jump to my own conclusions but rely on Your truth. Lord, I know that all my power comes from You. I am at Your feet, delivering all my worries and anxieties to You. They are a waste of time. I'm handing over my will, and I accept Your will in my life today.*

*All things are possible through my Lord and Savior, Jesus Christ!*

*In Jesus's name.*

*Amen.*

## Dear Lord,

*Forgive me when I allow weak thoughts to come into my head. And, Lord, let me forgive immediately those around me who may sin against You or me.*

*Lord, I humble myself before You. Through You is where I belong. Open my heart today to seek Your truth in all that I say and do. Let my heart and mind obey what Your plan is for me. And give me the peace to settle with Your plan. Lord, I ask You to guide me with Your grace and wisdom. Let me have patience to hold my tongue and train my thoughts to be mindful of Your presence, to be more like You, to trust in Your good and wonderful blessings on me, to encourage others with hope and humility today. Lord, it's in Your hands that I rest my heart and soul. In Jesus's powerful name, I pray.*

*Amen!*

## Dear Lord,

I am so grateful that You have chosen me. Sometimes when the pressures of the world are on me or things start to get out of hand, it's easy to forget one very important thing: You chose me to be Your light, to be an aware host to Your Holy Spirit, and to have an intimate relationship with You.

Lord, I'm asking for Your mighty strength and protection this week. I pray that Your Holy Spirit will guide my words and actions, that all will I feel is Your love, so I can show that same love to others. Even where the enemy is playing and scheming right now, let me be the light that shines in that darkness. Lord, You are my defender and savior. With You, anything is possible!

In Jesus's name.

Amen.

## Dear Lord,

*I am so humbled to have You with me. You have showed me Your grace and wisdom through this trip. Thank You for healing hearts and showing me trust and love for others when I thought I would never have it again. You've changed that love from being one that was out of obligation to a love that is so overwhelming. Thank You, Lord, for all Your blessings in my life. The bumpy road brought me to You. Your love conquers all! Please continue to open my heart, showing me everything You want me to see. Lord, give me Your continued grace and wisdom.*

*In Your name, I pray.*

*Amen.*

## Dear Lord,

*All the glory of whatever I do today is Yours. You are my rock and my salvation. You have shown me Your grace and mercy in all that I do. Come into my heart, Lord, and reveal to me all that I lack. I rebuke all that doesn't help me walk in Your footsteps or direct my path in the direction You want me to go. Light my way. Let me never doubt or worry about things that are never in my control, Lord. Help me deliver all of them to You.*

*Lord, bless those who are in my life and open their hearts to all Your goodness and love. Lord, let the Holy Spirit guide me to show others Your light. I declare that the Holy Spirit is breathing new life into miracles, healings, and wonders in the heavens and on earth.*

*In Jesus Christ's name, I pray.*

*Amen.*

> God is working in you, giving you the desire to obey Him and the power to do what pleases Him. (Philippians 2:13 NIV)

## Dear Lord,

*Thank You for Your love and Your blessings that are so great in my life.*

*Thank You that Your favor has no end. It keeps giving to me. Forgive me for not being patient and forgetting that You already know my ways intimately. You know what concerns me, and Your love always covers me like a shield.*

*I ask for Your guidance in everything I do so I can walk fully in Your blessings and goodness today. Open my eyes to see like You see. I ask that Your face shines on me. Open the right doors for my life and for my loved ones. Lord, let there be no limit to the love I give. Lord, I ask also that You close the doors that I should walk away from. Let me ultimately and without reserve trust in You. Establish the work for my hands to bring fulfillment to what You want me to do. I pray, Lord, that You make my steps purposeful and meaningful through Your goodness and love. Give me an open heart to Your wisdom to hear Your voice, and make me strong through Your unlimited favor and grace.*

*In Jesus Christ's name.*

Amen.

## Dear Lord,

*Forgive me of my impatience and frustrations. These feelings are so quick to surface in me. I know in my heart there is nothing I control. There is no situation that I can force to change for my own satisfaction.*

*Lord, let me think by the Spirit, let me speak by the Spirit, and let me live by the Spirit that lives in me.*

*Open my heart and my eyes to those in much more need than I am. Send me Your mercy and Your grace to fulfill Your path for my life. Send me the blessings You have, so that I may bless others and show them Your goodness. Lord, I pray that every child will see Your light and feel Your love today, so much that it changes their lives and points them to You. Lord, I rebuke all the enemy tries to do against them. Send only Your messengers and protect them with Your angel armies. Keep them innocent from the ways of the enemy, who tries to take control of their hearts and minds. Lead them away from the temptations that will only please their flesh and not their hearts. Show them the nourishment that only You can give. They are all Your children, Lord. Let me be Your light for them in their darkness.*

*In Jesus's name, I pray.*

*Amen.*

The Lord is faithful to all His promises and loving toward all he has made. (Psalm 145:13 NIV)

# Dear Lord,

Thank You for Your blessings. I know we are sometimes so caught up in the daily turmoil, and we can forget all that You have given us—all the blessings in our lives that would not be possible without You. Lord, let my faith in You never waver. Let it be tested in the fire and made stronger. Let me persevere to grow my faith stronger. Let the Holy Spirit show me what You have for me to do, in Your name.

Lord, I pray with my faith in You that the messages You want us to deliver today are found by those in need. The messages of hope and unending love to those who feel hopelessness. Let them be powerful enough through our faith in Your love. Let us be Your instruments, to be used by You and all for Your glory. Holy Spirit, guide each of us today so that it is only Your words that our tongues deliver to others, that only Your kindness, truth, and mercy come out. Cover us in the blood of Christ Jesus, washing us clean as snow today.

I ask this in Your Son's holy name.

Amen.

# Good morning, Lord.

*"Do not worry about anything, but pray about everything."*

*So simple yet so complicated. It sounds easy to do, but we always let the enemy drive, so worry always gets the shotgun seat. Lord, be with me now and help me see. Be real to me in my prayers.*

*Lord, I rebuke the enemy, who tries to steal my confidence. There is no room in me for shortsighted panic of things that will never happen. All that becomes wasted time and energy, time I won't get back. Lord, give me Your mercy to not be self-centered. Lord, thank You for this beautiful day. You will still tell the sun to rise, the birds will still sing, and the angels will still make the wind blow in the sky.*

*I believe that unseen goodness and love are more powerful than unseen chaos. Your goodness and love bring peace and love in my life.*

*Lord, let me choose the goodness and love today. Let me feel Your peace through the grace You give me. Give me Your wisdom to be a blessing to others today rather than focusing on myself and any chaos the enemy tries to create. God, You are in control! You are the one driving, and I am riding shotgun!*

*In Jesus's name.*

*Amen.*

## Dear Lord,

My faith in You is strong, yet there are times when I forget to let go of things that I cannot control. Lord, I ask You to open my heart and show me things I need to see, the things in me that I need to change. Worrying is not an option if my faith in You is pure. As a believer, I should stand confidently, serve compassionately, and speak carefully. As a believer, I should be what You want me to be, do what You want me to do, and always ask for Your Holy Spirit to speak through me. Let me be humble with the wisdom You give me.

In Jesus's name, I pray.

Amen.

## Dear Lord,

*Thank You for all Your blessings in my life. All the glory of these blessings go to You. I am nothing without Your grace. You are the rock that I am building my foundation on. The ways You direct me, guiding me to be closer to You, continue to fill me with Your hope and faith. Lord, You have shown me so many miracles in my life so I can see how You love me and that You are always near. It can be so easy to complain or become impatient and let the enemy speak doubt in our ears, but knowing You are near, that nothing happens without You, restores the faith and hope in me. Forgive me of any impatience. Thank You for the never-ending faith and love that You show me. Let me show others the hope that they can also have through You, through the light that shines in me.*

*Lord, open my heart today to absorb Your message You have for others, to hold on to the faith, love, and hope that only come from You.*

*In Jesus's name, I pray.*

*Amen.*

> For he has rescued us from the dominion of darkness
> and brought us into the kingdom of the son he loves,
> in whom we have redemption the forgiveness of sins.
> (Colossians 1:13 NIV)

# Dear Lord,

Let me be patient with others. Give me the knowledge and the wisdom to not react to things that happen that are out of my control but to stay in peace and patience.

Lord, I know I really have no control over anything, so help me to let go and turn things over to You.

Lord, please bless and protect those who are lost right now. Open their hearts to Your good Word. Help them to see the glory in You and the kingdom of light through Jesus Christ.

Lord, pick up in Your mighty hand Your good servants who need a place to rest. I know that each tear they shed You hold in Your hand.

Lord, this is a season of miracles. Please bless the hurt, the lost, and the tired with Your unfailing, never-ending love. Let Your light shine around them and give them peace that only comes from You.

In Jesus's name, I pray.

Amen.

## Dear Lord,

*Let me be faithful today. Through everything, let me always give You the glory first. Let me be thankful for all that You give me and don't give me. Lord, You have shown me Your grace and Your love for me. This time of year is not about us but everything for us. You gave us Your only Son to show us the most unselfish gift no one could ever understand, to be our Savior and forgive us, no matter what we have done. No gift is higher than the love You give us.*

*Lord, I am so grateful for all that You have done and will do in my life. I will praise You and thank You every day.*

*Lord, please show me where Your love is needed. Open my heart and my eyes that I may be able to see and hear those who need Your Word this season. It's not about me; it's all about You and what can be brought to those who need Your comfort and compassion. Teach me to look up and breathe in Your love.*

*In Jesus's name, I pray.*

Amen.

## Dear Lord,

Show me when my work becomes meaningless, when what I do every day isn't done in Your image and in the name of Your grace and glory. I praise You. Search my heart, Lord, and show me where I am less than what You want me to be.

Lord, let me be Your light. Show me that with You I can spread that light and shine it on others. Nothing is impossible with You. The true meaning of Your existence on earth was to spread Your love to those unloved and lost, to show us to have meaning in our actions so that others will follow and want to be more like You.

Lord, be with me today. Guide my footsteps to make each moment meaningful and dedicated to You. Let me receive Your words today to make meaningful actions. Thank You, Jesus!

In Jesus's name, I pray.

Amen.

## Dear Lord,

Give me the strength to have confidence through You and in all that You do. May I acknowledge You in everything that I do. My confidence isn't in what other people say to me but in what You say to me.

Lord, guide me today to be patient for Your message. Open my heart and mind to see You and to hear You. Don't let me push my own agenda. Life through Your salvation is so much greater than my own wants.

Give me the grace to hand over all my challenges and questions to You.

You are my provider and protector. "Your throne, O God, will last forever."

In Jesus's name.

Amen.

*What is hope? What is the true meaning of hope?*

*To us, the definition of hope isn't wishing something will happen.*

*Hope is the certainty of the present and the firm expectation for the future—no matter what and without doubt. Hope isn't linked with doubt. It's linked with faith, trust, and expectations.*

*With true hope, we don't question what we see. Instead, we have cause to do the following:*

*Praise God.*

*Rejoice.*

*Renew our strength.*

*Be inspired to live purely.*

*Be inspired to persevere.*

*Cure a downcast soul.*

*Never be disappointed.*

*Know that Your hope is a stabilizing anchor.*

*We always have this hope.*

# Dear Lord,

*Thank You for Your grace and wisdom today. Lord, let me consume You, Your words, and Your presence throughout today. I declare Your life in me.*

*Lord, teach me to know You as well as I know myself, to put my trust in You with all my heart. I refuse to settle for counterfeit joy that only promises momentary joy. Teach me to go deeper with You and learn the joy that only comes from You, not just to be cheerful or happy but to find joy in every circumstance.*

*Lord, I know Your words and only Your words that are spoken over me are true. Let Your words inhabit my heart and my soul. Let me find You in those moments when I think I'm lost and stand in Your truths.*

*In Jesus's name, I pray.*

*Amen.*

## Dear Lord,

*Give me hope without limits. Help me see the limits I have put on my life, the limits I have placed on my capabilities.*

*Help me to seek what is impossible every morning I wake up. Help me not to get stuck on only the tangible, to feel Your presence continually, not just in the mornings. Open my heart to the desire to seek it, to truly want it.*

*Hope tells me all things are possible. Faith will come from my hope, and I know true faith will lead to joy.*

*I believe that what could never happen can happen. I believe that what appears too good to be true can be true. Lord, You are without limits. Uncloud my mind that deters me from the limitless thinking.*

*Wake me up to see the more. Help me to see how big You really are. When I get afraid of the unknown of what lies ahead, show me how big You are. Let me dream that anything is possible when I call heaven down.*

*Lord, I pray with the authority that You gave me, to pray as a child who has no limitations. Stir me toward the hope that causes my spirit to awaken and live, that causes me to know that anything is possible through You.*

*I declare Your hope in me, Your power in me, and Your faith in me.*

*I pray for heaven to come down, for health and hope to consume me, for my mind to be limitless. I pray for the impossible to be possible. Fill me with the faith, hope, love, and dreams that reach beyond my imagination right now. I ask for more of You, Lord. I seek to find You and to receive all You have for me.*

*In Jesus's name, I pray.*

*Amen.*

The Lord is my strength and my defense.
(Exodus 15:2 NIV)

## Dear Lord,

*Thank You for this day You have given me, for being with me this morning.*

*Lord, be my strength today and let me give You my weaknesses. I know I can do all things through You. Show me how to pause before fear or doubt take hold in my mind. Help me to let go of the control and hand everything to You.*

*Lord, through Your power, I know nothing can keep a grip on me—not fear, worry, doubt, defeat, discouragement, loneliness, hardship, or pain.*

*I will adjust my stance from cowering to rising up. I will recognize and celebrate the power that is within my grasp, the hope that will never leave me.*

*I will speak the truth that all things can be done through Christ, and God will supply His perfect, never-ending power.*

*In Jesus's name, I pray.*

*Amen.*

# About the Author

Susan Maurer was born in San Diego, California, and raised in Texas. She came to know her faith in Texas in the midst of a normal, secular crisis. It was then that she knew there was more to her day-to-day life. Susan and her family moved to Florida, not knowing what they would find, but she knew that the Holy Spirit was urging her to move. Today, she works with a strip club ministry to help those who are vulnerable realize they too are loved. Susan considers her faith and family to be the most important aspects of her life.

Susan spends her worship time in the morning, writing the words she receives each morning from the Holy Spirit to bring hope to others. Each morning, she shares these prayers with many who feel lost or need to hear the words to know they are loved.

Susan is a wife, mother, and businesswoman of forty-two years, who felt the strong calling several years ago. Like most, it took many years of testing to truly understand the calling of her life. Susan was urged both by the women she ministers to and the Holy Spirit to publish these prayers.

It is her hope that these prayers will be used to touch the lives and hearts of others and give them the hope they need to stand firm and know they are loved.

Susan uses the trials and tribulations in her own life as the basis to relate to those who are lost or vulnerable. In her secular life, Susan wants to give back and show others that grace is given to all of us who believe in Jesus.

It is her hope that you take these words that the Holy Spirit has spoken and that they bring hope and light to your mornings.

Lightning Source UK Ltd.
Milton Keynes UK
UKHW011852080221
378458UK00001B/136